TREK

BY DAVID McCANDLESS

KT-433-126

TREKMASTER

BY DAVID McCANDLESS

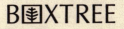
BOXTREE

First published in the UK in 1995 by
Boxtree Ltd
Broadwall House
21 Broadwall
London SE1 9PL

Copyright (c) Boxtree 1995

10 9 8 7 6 5 4 3 2

No part of this publication may be reproduced, stored in a retrieval
system or transmitted, in any form or by any means, electronic or
otherwise, without the express permission of the publisher

This publication is not licensed by, nor is Boxtree affiliated with
Paramount Pictures. This is a scholarly work intended to test the
knowledge of Star Trek fans.

Text Designed by Dan Newman
Headline font designed by James Sharer
Cover design by Colin Howard and Terry Rawlings at Classic Image

Cover photo – Range Pictures

Printed and bound in the UK by Cox and Wyman Ltd., Reading,
Berkshire

ISBN: 0 7522 0814 4

A CIP catalogue entry from the British Library

With special thanks to:

Captain James Clover
Captain Peter Ranson
Lieutenant Jason Parker
Ensign Kate O'Driscoll
Cadet Kathy Lozito
Admiral Callie Spiner
Lieutenant Matt Evans
Cadet Anne Davenport
Cadet Terry Preshaw
Cadet Diane L. Williams
Cadet Simon Coury
Lieutenant Commander Jake Lingwood

So, you think you know your Trek huh?
We'll see...

RULES

The TrekMaster rules are, as you would expect from a quiz of this splendour, very simple. The main thing to consider is difficulty level. Don't over-estimate your ability. Some questions are easy, some are hard, and some have been conceived by Satan Himself. Generally speaking, each section is split into three difficulty levels:

ENSIGN

For dabblers and closet Trekkers. You've seen a few episodes, but not in any order or under any strict regime. You've flicked tentatively through a few books in Forbidden Planet, but you've been too embarrassed to buy. You're probably a closet Trekker. You watch, hire, and buy but you don't admit to it. You know Spock's father's name, but not his brother's. You know Picard was born in France but don't know exactly where. And you probably know that DS9 was built by the Cardassians, but you don't know what they called it.

CAPTAIN

A strong healthy paragon of Trekdom. You're the kind of person who keeps Trek alive. You know your stuff but you're no big head. You've seen every episode of CT, TNG and DS9, and you're pretty savvy on plot lines, episode names, and those little character foibles which make Trek so watchable. You've got a tough task ahead of you though. The path to Captaincy is strewn with pitfalls and rogue quantum filaments. If you're Trek enough, you might just make it.

ADMIRAL

Now you're talking. Those who attempt Admiral difficulty are supreme Trekkers. You've seen every episode and film three or four times. You've read all the books and maybe even watched that dire 25th Anniversary film thing. You know Worf's family better than your own. You know who Flint, Captain Bozeman, Dr. Reyga, and Neela are. Hell, you live, eat, drink, sleep, and dream Trek. You probably hire *Excalibur* every other weekend just to see your idol, Patrick Stewart, in a skirt. You are a contender for the ultimate accolade – TrekMaster. Good luck. (You'll need it.)

The multiple choice questions at the start of some sections are just there to give you a taste of what to expect from the section and difficulty level, and to warn off young cadets who think they'll go straight for Admiralcy. As if.

SCORING

If you're playing on your own, the scoring works thus:

Two points for a completely correct answer. For example, for a full episode name rather than a potted plot description, an accurate character name as opposed to a mispronunciation, and a full description of somebody's title [i.e. Timcin's daughter, Dana] instead of a half-baked reply.

One point for a reasonably accurate answer. Getting close to a numerical answer, an accurate description of a character rather than their name, a mispronunciation, and stuff like that. Use your discretion.

One point for each part of a multi-part question. For instance, when Q transports the crew to Sherwood Forest in Q-Pid, you'll get a point for each crew member you successfully match up with each of Robin Hood's henchmen.

Ten bonus points for getting every question within a section correct at *every* skill level. A very rare occurrence so you should be rewarded.

If you're playing on your own do each section one by one and write the answers down on a piece of paper. Don't look at the answer after every question – the answers can often reveal another answer to a later question.

ALTERNATIVE RULES

Of course the best way to play TrekMaster is with a group of your Trek 'chums'. Closet Trekkers may have a problem here, but there are a few seedy bars in London which will rectify this. In the meantime, here are a few 'ideas' for more interesting TrekMastering.

ONE ON ONE
A competition between you and your best 'pal' to see who is the Trekkiest. You take turns to be QuestionMaster and choose a range of varied topics. Of course, this is just an excuse for the Question Master to be as supercilious and evil as possible [not letting your chum 'have' a question, penalising for vague answers, and then calling them a 'thickie' if they get a stupendously easy question wrong, etc]. Be warned, however, the more of a Jeremy Paxton you are as the Question Master, the more likely your chum will be too, and the more likely the whole game will spiral into name-calling and, eventually, a fist fight or a mud-wrestle or something.

TREKSTERMIND

Best with three or more players, Trekstermind follows the format of the TV show of a similar name. Each person chooses a 'specialist subject' [Data's Personal Log, CT Episodes, etc] and must answer as many questions as possible within two minutes [make sure you have a score keeper and somebody with a watch]. In the second round, a random section is chosen for each candidate. And then, in the third round, it's just straight general Trek knowledge, plucked from Pot Pourri rounds. This is a great way to while away the evenings, and for extra drama, sit each contestant on a chair in the middle of the room and shine a standard lamp in their face.

TREK TRIVIA

By far and away the best method for playing TrekMaster is to use an average common or garden Trivia board [every household has one gathering dust somewhere]. Play using the same rules, singly or in teams of two or three, but just swap the subjects likes this:

COLOUR	PREVIOUS SUBJECT	NEW SUBJECT
Blue	Geography	ALIENS
Pink	Entertainment	THE SERIES
Yellow	History	CT
Brown	Art & Literature	DS9
Green	Science & Nature	TNG
Orange	Sport & Leisure	ACADEMY EXAM

ABBREVIATIONS USED IN THIS BOOK

CT	Classic Trek
TNG	The Next Generation
DS9	Deep Space
SFA	Starfleet Academy
ST I	The Motion Picture
ST II	The Wrath of Khan
ST III	The Search for Spock
ST IV	The Voyage Home
ST V	The Final Barrier
ST VI	The Undiscovered Country
STG	Generations

CLASSIC TREK

CLASSIC TREK

MULTIPLE CHOICE
answers page 160

ENSIGN

1   What is Spock's reaction in *Amok Time* when he realises he
    hasn't actually killed Captain Kirk?
    a) He raises an eyebrow and says, 'Fascinating.'
    b) He has no reaction.
    c) He smiles and shouts 'Jim!'.

2   What is Dr. McCoy's nickname?
    a) Doc.
    b) Bones.
    c) Boney.

3   In which CT episode do we first meet the Romulans?
    a) *Day Of The Dove.*
    b) *Amok Time.*
    c) *Balance Of Terror.*

CAPTAIN

4   Where do the United Federation of Planets and the Klingons
    meet to reconcile their differences in *Errand of Mercy*?
    a) Organia.
    b) Ceti Alpha VI.
    c) Earth.

5   Why did the android Rayna kill herself in *Requiem*?
    a) Because she was in love with Flint.
    b) Because she was in love with Kirk.
    c) Because she was in love with Spock.

6   What plague has struck the crew in *Requiem For Methuselah*?
    a) Tamarian Plasma Plague.
    b) Klingon flu.
    c) Rigellian Fever.

ADMIRAL

7 Chekov, under the influence of an alien being in *Day Of The Dove*, believes he has a what?
a) A sister.
b) A brother.
c) A son.

8 Which deck are Kirk's quarters on?
a) Deck Five.
b) Deck Six.
c) Deck Seven.

9 What did McCoy accidentally leave behind on the planet in *A Piece Of The Action*?
a) A book about gangsters.
b) His phaser.
c) His communicator.

ENTERPRISE CREW

answers page 160

ENSIGN

1 What type of officer wears a red uniform?

2 What is Yeoman Rand's first name?

3 Who was Mr. Kyle in CT?

4 What is Mr. Scott's parting gift to the Klingons in *The Trouble With Tribbles?*

5 What finally provokes Scotty into a fight with the Klingons in the same episode?

6 What is Chekov's first name?

7 What rank is Chekov in CT?

8 Who is the only crew member unaffected by the spores in *This Side Of Paradise*?

9 Who was rejected as a host by the salt vampire?

10 Who is accused of murder in *Wolf In The Fold*?

CAPTAIN

11 Who are captured by the Romulans in *The Enterprise Incident*?

12 Why does Uhura have to learn to read in *The Changeling*?

13 How does the crew overcome the rampant computer in *I, Mudd*?

14 Who flies the shuttlecraft inside the monster-alien in *The Immunity Syndrome*?

15 What does the uninhibited Mr. Sulu do in *The Naked Time*?

16 Which two crew members are turned into 'zombies' in *Catspaw*?

17 Which four crew members are stranded in an alternate universe in *Mirror, Mirror*?

18 Which parallel-Enterprise crew member helps them?

19 How does Scotty overcome his Kelvan?

20 Who objects to Apollo's interest in Lieutenant Carolyn Palamas?

21 Which alternate crew members attempted to assassinate the alternate Kirk?

ADMIRAL

22 How did the crew wrestle back control of the Enterprise from the Kelvans in *By Any Other Name*?

23 What is Sulu's hobby?

24 Which CT episode did Chekov first appear in?

25 Who is Chekov's ex girlfriend in *Way To Eden*?

26 What is Chekov's middle name?

27 Who is struck by the ray in in *Return Of The Archons*?

28 Why was Chekov unaffected by the ageing disease in *The Deadly Years*?

CHARACTERS

answers page 160

ENSIGN

1 Who developed *The Ultimate Computer*?

2 Who was the real murderer in *Wolf In The Fold*?

3 In *The Apple*, the inhabitants of Gamma Trianguli VI are called the "Feeders Of Vaal" – what exactly is Vaal?

4 Why does Pike return to the Talosians in *The Menagerie*?

5 What does Harry Mudd trade in?

6 What is the name of the old earth probe determined to destroy all 'imperfect' life forms in *The Changeling*?

7 Which eugenics superman took control of the Enterprise?

8 What does the alien creature in *Man Trap* crave?

9 What did 20th century Earth society call Redjac?

10 What happened to Sarek on board the Enterprise-A in *Journey To Babel*?

11 Why did Kollos the Medusan have to travel in a box in *Is There No Truth In Beauty*?

12 What is Harry Mudd's full name?

CAPTAIN

13 Who is the captain of the U.S.S. Constellation?

14 Why does the rock-eating Horta attack the miners in

Devil In The Dark?

15 Who was Mr. Flint?

16 Which CT character in *The Square Of Gothos* closely resembles Q in TNG?

17 Which alien was so ugly, just his look could kill?

18 Why did Nomad want to exterminate all mankind?

19 Why did Deela commandeer the Enterprise in *Wink Of An Eye*?

20 Why did Mudd have an android of his nagging wife built?

21 What did the inhabitants of Antos IV teach Captain Garth (as revealed in *Whom Gods Destroy*)?

22 What unfortunate side-effect did this have on him?

ADMIRAL

23 What has Federation Cultural Observer John Gill recreated on Ekos in *Patterns Of Force*?

24 But who is the power behind the throne of John Gill?

25 What is the name of the nefarious trader who sells Tribbles?

26 Why does Finney fake his own death in *Court-Martial*?

27 Which captain is in search of eternal youth in *The Omega Glory*?

28 What biological difference is there between humans and the humanoid Apollo in *Who Mourns For Adonais*?

29 Who conducts Spock's marriage ceremony in *Amok Time*?

30 Which gladiator were Bones and Spock forced to fight in *Bread and Circuses*?

31 Why did Kodos the Executioner order the deaths of 4,000 of his people?

32 Why was Flint slowly dying in *Requiem For Methuselah*?

PLOTS

answers page 161

ENSIGN

1 When did the children on Miri's planet usually die?

2 How does the planet Iotia come to be modelled on 1920s Chicago in *A Piece Of The Action*?

3 What does the M-5 computer do wrong?

4 Who was actually carrying out the murders Anton Karidian was suspected of in *Conscience Of The King*?

5 Why?

6 How do the aliens in *The Cage* communicate?

7 What Earth time period is focused on in *Bread And Circuses*?

8 What does the death of the Tribbles who ate the grain reveal?

9 What happens to the crew members who beam down to Gamma Hydra IV in *The Deadly Years*?

10 What did the Orkirohium Cloud Creature feed on in *Obsession*?

11 How does the Enterprise remove Apollo's source of power?

12 What does the Enterprise find on an Earth-like planet in *Miri*?

13 Which greek philosopher did the inhabitants of the planet ruled by Parmen base their culture on?

14 What emotion did Redjac feed on in *Wolf In The Fold*?

CAPTAIN

15 What are "The Lights of Zetar"?

16 Who are arming one side of a conflict in *A Private Little War*?

17 Why have the Kelvans come to this galaxy in *By Any Other Name*?

18 What had killed the crew of the other Starfleet vessel in *Omega Glory*?

19 Why don't the children of Triacus show any emotion at the death of the parents in *And The Children Shall Lead*?

20 What is the only consistent thing in Pike's visions in *The Cage*?

21 What profession of people did Mudd sell his women to in *Mudd's Women*?

22 Who are trying to form an alliance with the Capellans in *Friday's Child*?

23 How do they end up in the parallel universe?

24 How did Captain Decker attempt to save his crew from the planet killer?

25 Why did this plan fail?

26 How did he attempt to suicidally destroy the machine?

27 Did he succeed?

28 How did the Enterprise crew capitalise on his failure?

29 Did it work?

30 In *Operation: Annihilate!* the planet Deneva, where Kirk's family live, is under threat from what?

31 What did the alien entity in *Day Of The Dove* force the Klingons and the Enterprise crew to do?

32 Why?

33 What happens to Mudd at the end of *I, Mudd*?

34 What are the aliens using the empath for in *The Empath*?

35 What did the mega computer Landru do to the surviving members of the U.S.S. Archon in *Return Of The Archons*?

36 What was wrong with the Eden found by Dr.Sevrin in Romulan space?

ADMIRAL

37 Why are the gangsters in *A Piece Of The Action* so interested in the Enterprise?

38 Why, in reality, are the miners working on Stratos less intelligent than the upper class living in the clouds?

39 What is threatening a planet in *The Paradise Syndrome*?

40 Which type of emotion acts as a barrier against the Talosians' mind-reading in *The Cage*?

41 How do Mudd's women maintain their youth?

42 What do the 'sun' worshippers in *Bread And Circuses* actually worship?

43 Why didn't the crew who beamed down from the Enterprise in *City On The Edge Of Forever* disappear when the future was changed and the ship ceased to exist?

44 What do the highly advanced alien brains offer in exchange for borrowing the crew's bodies in *The Gamesters Of Triskelion*?

45 Who is Edith Keeler's favourite film star?

46 What is deadly to the parasitic bat-like aliens in *Operation: Annhilate*?

47 What exactly is *The Corbomite Maneuver*?

48 How did agents 201 and 347 die in *Assignment: Earth*?

OBSERVATION

answers page 161

ENSIGN

1 The *Conscience Of The King* revolves around which playwright's plays?

2 What two things happen to the crew members affected by the energy barrier in *Where No Man Has Gone Before?*

3 What did the frightening Balok in *The Corbomite Maneuver* actually look like?

4 What does the entrance to Vaal look like?

5 What is the Enterprise mistaken for when it is accidentally thrown back to the year 1969?

6 What do the bored aliens in *The Gamesters Of Triskelion* look like?

7 How does Apollo first appear to the Enterprise crew in *Who Mourns For Adonais?*

CAPTAIN

8 Which two stalwarts of McCoy and Spock were first introduced in *The Enemy Within?*

9 Which weapon appeared in *Where No Man Has Gone Before* but never again in any CT episode?

10 What was the full name of the Enterprise in the alternate universe in *Mirror, Mirror?*

11 What is Harry Mudd's nagging wife called in *I, Mudd?*

12 What does the huge monster alien in *The Immunity Syndrome* look like?

13 What were changed into swords in *Day Of The Dove?*

ADMIRAL

14 What will the son of Captain Christopher in *Tomorrow Is Yesterday* do?

15 What is the oldest relic any Trek crew has come across?

16 What was Landru's planet's populace called?

17 What are the majority of the crew turned into in *By Any Other Name*?

18 How long was the Horta's cycle of rebirth in *Devil In The Dark*?

19 Name the recreated mythological figures who appear on the planet Excalbia in *The Savage Curtain*?

20 How long had the computer-simulated war lasted in *A Taste Of Armageddon*?

CAPTAIN JAMES T. KIRK: PERSONAL LOG

answers page 162

ENSIGN

1 What does the T in James T stand for?

2 Who is Kirk's eugenic superman of an adversary?

3 How does Charlie X come to regard Kirk?

4 In *Arena*, the powerful Metrons force Kirk and a Gorn captain to… what?

5 How does Kirk appear to die under Spock's hand in *Amok Time*?

6 What does Kirk teach Sahna the meaning of in *Gamesters Of Triskelion*?

7 What does Kirk use to overcome Khan?

8 How does Kirk propose to stop Bele possessing the Enterprise in

Let That Be Your Last Battlefield?

CAPTAIN

9 Why did Kirk allow Edith Keeler to die?

10 How many bands does Kirk wear on his arm?

11 Who does the bad Kirk attack in *The Enemy Within*?

12 Why does Kirk faces court martial in *Court Martial*?

13 What was so special about Kirk when he won command of the Enterprise?

14 What is Kirk obsessed by in *Obsession*?

15 Why does the Gideon Prime Minister Hodin steal Kirk in the *Mark Of Gideon*?

16 Which historical figure is Kirk's idol?

17 In which episode does Kirk get married?

18 Why?

ADMIRAL

19 Which scientist takes over Kirk's body?

20 What is her relationship to Kirk?

21 Where was Kirk born?

22 What is the name of Kirk's brother?

23 But what does Jim call him?

24 How does Kirk violate Capellan tradition in *Friday's Child*?

25 Who does the Nomad probe mistake Kirk for in *The Changeling*?

26 How does Kirk dissolve the threat of Nomad?

27 How does Kirk convince Nomad that it is imperfect in *The Changeling*?

28 How did Gary Mitchell once save Kirk's life (as related in *Where No Man Has Gone Before*)?

SCIENCE OFFICER SPOCK: PERSONAL LOG

answers page 162

ENSIGN

1 What caused Spock to fall in love in *This Side Of Paradise*?

2 Who is Spock's father?

3 What position does he hold in Starfleet?

4 Which CT character confessed her love for Spock?

5 Which physical feature distinguished the alternate Spock from the real Spock in *Mirror, Mirror*?

6 How does Spock save himself from blindness after McCoy bathes him in intense light to kill a parasitic alien using Spock as a host in *Operation: Annhilate!*?

7 Who does Spock's 'fiancée' choose as his opponent in *Amok Time*?

CAPTAIN

8 Why does Spock turn traitor in *The Enterprise Incident*?

9 Why does the first glimpse of Romulans create problems for Spock?

10 What does Spock manage to build using 1930s technology in *City On The Edge Of Forever*?

11 Why does Spock refuse be a blood donor to his father in *Journey To Babel*?

12 What did the Controllers steal from Spock?

13 Why?

14 Why is Spock so alienated from his father?

15 In which episode is Spock seen holding a human baby?

ADMIRAL

16 What is the name of Spock's mother?

17 What is the name of Spock's half-brother?

18 How does Spock manage to get the damaged shuttle into orbit in *The Galileo Seven*?

19 What was Spock's pet as a child?

20 How does Spock know that the U.S.S. Intrepid has been destroyed at the beginning of *The Immunity Syndrome*?

21 How many times has Spock's father been married?

22 What blood type do Spock and his father share?

23 What is the name of Spock's wife-to-be in *Amok Time*?

DOCTOR McCOY: PERSONAL LOG

answers page 162

ENSIGN

1 What is Bones' full name?

2 What method of transport does McCoy hate?

3 What is the antidote to the accelerating ageing the crew encounter in *The Deadly Years*?

CAPTAIN

4 What is the name of the old sweetheart McCoy meets up with in *The Man Trap*?

5 What was her nickname for him?

6 How does McCoy describe himself?

ADMIRAL

7 How does Bones unintentionally violate a tribal taboo in *Friday's Child*?

8 What 'kills' McCoy in *Shore Leave*?

9 What does McCoy accidentally do at the beginning of *City On The Edge Forever*?

EPISODES

answers page 162

1 In which episode do the Klingons and The Enterprise join forces to overcome an alien who feeds on their hatred?

2 Which CT episode was remade in TNG as *The Naked Now*?

3 In which episode is an amnesiac Kirk taken in by a village of red indians?

4 In which episode does a Greek God appear?

5 In which episode do Kirk, Bones and Spock beam down to the library of a dying planet?

6 In which episode does Spock mindmeld with a silicon slug?

7 Which episode saw the first use of the Vulcan death grip?

8 In which episode does McCoy deliver an alien baby?

9 Which episode links CT to DS9?

10 In which episode do Kirk and Spock fight Nazis?

11 Which episode sees Spock fall in love?

12 In which episode is Kirk split into a good and evil version of himself?

13 In which episode does McCoy contract a fatal illness?

14 In which episode is Scotty under suspicion of murder?

15 In which episode does Kirk arm one side of a faction to maintain a balance of power?

16 In which episode does Harry Mudd first appear?

17 In which episode do Kirk, McCoy, Spock, and Chekov fight it out at the OK Corral?

18 In which episode is there a race with a caste system, the highest of which live on a cloud?

19 In which episode does Kirk meet Abraham Lincoln?

20 In which episode does the Enterprise encounter lifeforms which exists in an 'accelerated time frame'?

21 Which episode is set in a society based on the gangster period of 1920s Chicago?

22 In which episode does Spock go through 'pon farr'?

23 In which episode do half-black/half-white and half-white/half-black fight it out?

24 Which CT episode uses footage from the unscreened pilot, *The Cage*?

25 In which episode is the Enterprise a 'casualty' in an on-going nuclear war?

26 In which episode does Spock take control of the Enterprise and face court-martial?

27 Which episode is set inside a haunted house?

28 In which episode do Kirk and the crew find the inventor of the warp drive?

29 Which episode first features Spock's father?

30 In which episode is a prototype mega-computer given a test run on the Enterprise-A?

31 Name two episodes in which Scotty is 'in love'.

32 What was the name of the last ever episode of CT?

THE NEXT GENERATION

THE NEXT GENERATION

MULTIPLE CHOICE

answers page 163

ENSIGN

1   Why do Klingons howl during their death ritual?
a) To cast off any evil thoughts before dying.
b) To warn the dead that a Klingon warrior is coming.
c) Because they are upset.

2   Riva's three aides in *Loud As A Whisper* represent which aspects of his character?
a) Passion, intellect, and harmony.
b) Anger, love, and reason.
c) Extremity, passion, and lust.

3   Why does Worf faint in *Up The Long Ladder*?
a) The bridge becomes too hot for him.
b) He sees a dead body.
c) He is suffering from Klingon flu.

4   Who does Lwaxana Troi say she is going to marry in *Manhunt*?
a) Picard.
b) Riker.
c) Geordi.

5   *The Host* opens with Bev and Troi having what?
a) A giggle.
b) Beauty treatment.
c) A haircut.

6   What does Picard do to relax in *The Big Goodbye*?
a) He goes riding on the holodeck.
b) He plays a detective on the holodeck.
c) He visits a jazz bar on the holodeck.

CAPTAIN

7 What was Masaka the god of?
   a) The Earth
   b) The Sun.
   c) The Moon

8 Next to Data's off switch are some other buttons. What are they?
   a) His internal chronometer.
   b) His reset button.
   c) His access terminals.

9 What is standard Starfleet procedure for a captain who has lost a ship?
   a) He is imprisoned until trial.
   b) He is court-martialled.
   c) He is demoted.

10 Lwaxana Troi is heir to what?
   a) The Fifth House of Betazed.
   b) The Holy Rings of Betazed.
   c) The Crowned Sceptre of Betazed.

11 How does Guinan test Q's new-found mortality in *Deja Q*?
   a) She hits him.
   b) She pours a drink over his head.
   c) She stabs him with a fork.

12 In which episode do we first see Guinan?
   a) *The Child*.
   b) *Evolution*.
   c) *The Neutral Zone*.

ADMIRAL

13 What is Picard's assumed name in *Gambit*?
   a) Gaylen.
   b) Daren.
   c) Boran.

14 Admiral Quinn brought a rather horrible worm-like alien thing on board the Enterprise in *Conspiracy*. Who was it for?
   a) Picard.
   b) Riker.
   c) Beverly Crusher.

15 In which episode does Wesley get his first kiss?
a) *The Game*.
b) *The Dauphin*.
c) *Coming Of Age*.

16 What instrument does Data regularly play?
a) The fiddle.
b) The viola.
c) The violin.

17 What does 'Darmok on the ocean' describe?
a) Being at sea.
b) Being on a starship.
c) Being alone.

18 Who are *The Survivors*?
a) Kevin and Rishon Uxbridge.
b) A little boy and his mother.
c) Two Romulans.

THE CREW IN PERIL

answers page 163

ENSIGN

1 How does the Enterprise get out of a Romulan trap in *The Defector*?

2 What is responsible for the ships problems in *Evolution*?

3 Which crew members does Moriarty kidnap?

4 What happens to the Enterprise in *Cause And Effect*?

5 Who is apparently in the process of being shot by a disrupter when time is frozen in *Timescape*?

6 How does the Enterprise escape from within the asteroid in *The Pegasus*?

7 What happens to the crew of the Enterprise in *Remember Me*?

CAPTAIN

8 How does the entity in *Where Silence Has Lease* check whether humans are mortals?

9 How does a Klingon hold the Enterprise to ransom in *Heart Of Glory*?

10 Which race interrupts the Enterprise's battle exercises in *Peak Performance*?

11 Why is Picard sent on a dangerous secret away mission in *Chain Of Command*?

12 Who joins him on said dangerous away mission?

13 Which two crew members are kidnapped by terrorists in *The High Ground*?

14 In *Masks*, the Enterprise starts to turn into what?

ADMIRAL

15 Why couldn't Beverly save Tasha Yar's life?

16 What is noticeable about the virus in *Angel One*?

17 How many times is the Enterprise destroyed in *Cause And Effect*?

18 What causes *Disaster*?

19 In which episode does the Enterprise use a solar flare to destroy an enemy ship?

20 Which tactic is employed to save the Enterprise in *Disaster*, *Cause And Effect* and *Galaxy's Child*?

21 What is a new medical condition named, after it rampages through the crew in *Genesis*?

22 Name three episodes in which the Enterprise is seen to be destroyed.

OBJECTS

answers page 163

ENSIGN

1 What colour is the model of the Stargazer in Picard's ready room?

2 What is *The Royale*?

3 Why was it constructed?

4 What does the mind control device in *The Battle* look like?

5 What is a metagenic weapon?

6 What object do the time-travelling aliens in *Time's Arrow* concentrate their power into?

CAPTAIN

7 What is a Samarian Sunset?

8 What was the name of the super-computer which ran the planet Aldea in *When The Bough Breaks*?

9 What is the name of the maintenance-robots-cum-accidentally-sentient-life-forms in *Quality Of Life*?

10 Name two objects Rasmussen steals in *A Matter Of Time*?

11 What is the Mask of Masaka?

ADMIRAL

12 What is a Glavin?

13 What is strange about the US flag the crew beam aboard in *The Royale*?

14 What does the Tox Uthat actually do?

15 What is the 'Kurlan Naiskos'?

answers page 164

ENSIGN

1   A picture of what hangs in Picard's ready room?

2   In the first season of TNG users of the holodeck had to say what to reveal the exit of the holodeck?

3   What does the picture in Sickbay depict?

4   How old was Dr. McCoy in *Encounter At Farpoint*?

5   What race did the Mintakans closely resemble in *Who Watches The Watchers*?

6   What do the stranded crew members look like in the transporter beam in *Realm Of Fear*?

7   How many Romulans were actually interdimensional aliens in *Timescape*?

8   How many times has the Enterprise's saucer section been separated and in which episodes?

CAPTAIN

9   How long is the ship's destruct sequence set for in *11001001*?

10 Which Federation ship is destroyed in *Conspiracy*?

11 What percentage of the Borg ship does the Enterprise manage to destroy in *Q-Who*?

12 How many Borgs transport onto the Enterprise in *Q-Who*?

13 What did the crew dub the alien lifeform who mistook the Enterprise for its mother in *Galaxy's Child*?

14 How far in the future does the shuttle come from in *Time Squared*?

15 What ships do the Ferengi pilot in *Rascals*?

16 What play was Mr. Picard's theatre group rehearsing in 19th century San Francisco?

17 What did the victims of the time-travelling life-force-sucking aliens in *Time's Arrow* appear to have died from?

18 In *The Inner Light* Picard lives an entire life in how many minutes of Enterprise time?

19 In *Sub Rosa*, we find out an alien entity has been in Beverly Crusher's family for how many years?

20 In which episode do we first see the officers playing poker?

ADMIRAL

21 What is the registration number of the Enterprise's sister ship, the Yamato?

22 In *Elementary, My Dear Data*, which ship is the Enterprise waiting to rendezvous with?

23 When did Spock first meet Pardek?

24 Who was the chief engineer before Geordi in the first season of TNG?

25 In *The Drumhead* how many times is Picard said to have broken the prime directive?

26 How many cryogenic chambers are empty of the derelict Earth ship in *The Neutral Zone*?

27 Which ship's crew is completely wiped out by the deadly ageing virus in *Unnatural Selection*?

28 Roughly how many light years did the Enterprise travel in *Nth Degree*?

29 In *Q-Who*, the Enterprise is flung hundreds of light years into the Delta Quadrant. How long would it have taken the Enterprise to reach the nearest star base (approximately)?

30 In *Yesterday's Enterprise*, how long has the alternate Enterprise been at war with the Klingons?

31 How long was the Enterprise trapped in *Cause And Effect*?

32 Name two places in which the number '3' appears in *Cause And Effect*?

33 What does Data say Picard will more than likely change into in *Genesis*?

34 What is Picard's Aunt Adel's cure for colds?

35 What is Picard's Aunt Adel's cure for insomnia?

36 Where is the spatial anomaly in *All Good Things…*?

THE ENTERPRISE CREW

answers page 164

ENSIGN

1 Who is the Enterprise's barber?

2 Who follows Worf in the chain of command?

3 Who is the best shuttle pilot on the Enterprise?

4 Who is the best poker player on the Enterprise?

5 Which crew member does Spot particularly hate?

6 Which crew member does Spot particularly like?

7 What happened to Guinan's race?

8 What is Tasha Yar's first name?

9 Who keeps a saddle in their quarters?

10 Who is trapped on a downed shuttle craft in *Skin Of Evil*?

11 Why did the crew beam down to the planet in *Skin Of Evil*?

12 Which three characters form the *Ménage A Troi*?

13 In whose quarters do the holodeck characters Moriarty and his countess reside?

14 Who hears voices in *Cause And Effect*?

15 In *The Mind's Eye*, who is kidnapped and brainwashed by the Romulans?

16 Who assumes the role of captain after the ship-wide memory loss in *Conundrum*?

17 Which three characters are possessed by aliens in *Power Play*?

18 *Nth Degree* sees which crew member turned into a super-genius?

19 What is Wes's nickname for Mr. Barclay in *Hollow Pursuits*?

20 Which two crew members travel to Romulus in *Unification*?

21 Which four characters are turned into children in *Rascals*?

22 Who worked together to crack the Romulan progressive encryption lock in *Unfication II*?

23 What did the officers of the Enterprise-D pretend to be in 19th century San Francisco?

24 Which famous author do the crew meet in 19th century San Francisco?

25 Which famous crew member do the crew meet in 19th century San Francisco?

26 Who joins Alexander and Worf on the holodeck in *A Fistful Of Datas*?

27 Who become *Attached*?

28 What unusual ability does this give them?

29 In *Lower Decks*, Ensign Ravell is basically a younger version of who?

30 In *Emergence*, whose program is the Orient Express?

31 Which crew member returns on *Pre-emptive Strike*?

32 How and in which episode was Tasha Yar killed?

CAPTAIN

33 In which two episodes does Ensign Sito Jaxa appear?

34 How does she die?

35 How does Picard test her mettle?

36 Who is next in command after Picard and Riker?

37 In *Code Of Honour*, Tasha Yar is kidnapped and forced to what?

38 What befalls Picard and Crusher on the planet Minos in *Arsenal Of Freedom*?

39 How do Riker, Worf and Data escape the Hotel Royale?

40 Who requests Moriarty's creation on the Holodeck?

41 What mistake did he make in doing so?

42 Which crew member enthusiastically aids and abets the distinctly doolally Admiral Satie in *The Drumhead*?

43 Who is the only crew member to suspect an anomaly in *Yesterday's Enterprise*?

44 Who leads the mutiny against 'the captain' in *Allegiance*?

45 Who does Barclay beat up on the holodeck at the beginning of *Hollow Pursuits*?

46 Who played Cyrano De Bergerac on the Enterprise?

47 What actually are the 'ghosts' which possess crew members in *Power Play*?

48 Which two crew members are given commands of their own ships in *Redemption II*?

49 Which crew member beams over to try to placate Captain Ben Maxwell in *The Wounded*?

50 Who suffers from transporter phobia?

51 Who wrote the play *Frame Of Mind*?

52 Who go out of phase in *The Next Phase*?

53 Who first experiences the time distortion in *Timescape*?

54 What kind of animal does Barclay become when the crew de-evolve in *Genesis*?

55 Which two crew members travel into Data's dreams in *Phantasms*?

56 In *Journey's End*, the Enterprise crew encounter which Earth culture?

ADMIRAL

57 Which Vulcan doctor occasionally appears in TNG?

58 How many times has Dr. Pulaski been married?

59 How old was Tasha Yar when she was abandoned on Turkana 4?

60 Which part does Guinan play in Picard's Dixon Hill stories?

61 Who brings back the contagion in *The Naked Now*?

62 In *Coming Of Age*, Mr. Kerland steals a shuttle. Why?

63 What is the name of the evil in *Skin Of Evil*?

64 How many people attended Tasha's funeral?

65 Who makes the first contact with *Angel One*?

66 Why?

67 Why is Data the only crew member sent down to convince colonists to evacuate in *The Ensigns Of Command*?

68 In *Q-Who*, who spills hot chocolate on Captain Picard?

69 What is the name of the new executive officer who appears after the crew loses its memory in *Conundrum*?

70 Who volunteers to host Odan in *The Host*?

71 What IQ does Barclay claim to have in *Nth Degree*?

72 In *Q-Pid*, the crew of the Enterprise are turned into characters from Robin Hood. Who plays who?

73 How do Picard, Data and Spock escape from Sela in *Unification II*?

74 How do the crew know the bomb in *Reunion* was of Romulan design?

75 Who wrist has been broken in *Clues*?

76 Who do the Paxons take over in *Clues*?

77 In *Night Terrors*, the crew suffer from a lack of what?

78 What musical instrument is Nella Daren 'good at' in *Lessons*?

79 Whereabouts on the Enterprise do Daren and Picard have a 'gig' in *Lessons*?

80 What does hypochondriac Barclay think he's contracted in *Genesis*?

81 Which officer particularly likes Ensign Sito in *Lower Decks*?

82 Where has Ro apparently been for two years in *Pre-Emptive Strike*?

83 In which episode do we first see Guinan?

CHARACTERS

answers page 165

ENSIGN

1 What is Moriarty's first name?

2 Who was Sherlock Holmes' police inspector friend?

3 Who is Tasha's daughter?

4 What happens to Admiral Jameson as the episode *Too Short A Season* unfolds?

5 How did he break the prime directive?

6 What does Anya, the bodyguard of dauphin Salia in *The Dauphin*, insist Pulaski do to an infected patient?

7 What rank was *The Defector*?

8 What did he do when he realised he had been set up?

9 Who is Riva?

10 Why is Roga Danar able to escape the Enterprise's capture for so long?

11 What do Alexander and Troi's mother share in *Costs Of Living*?

12 What is the name of the goddess who returns to claim her planet in *Devil's Due*?

13 K'Ehleyr said she had inherited her mother's sense of humour and her father's...?

14 Who is Kamala, *The Perfect Mate*, attracted to?

15 Which DS9 character pops up in *Firstborn*?

16 A 'Takesian Razor Beast' is whose imaginary friend?

17 How does Moriarty leave the holodeck?

CAPTAIN

18 Why is Tasha Yar's sister so eager to join the Enterprise's away team in _Legacy_?

19 Why has the _Tin Man_ come to a dying star?

20 What race is Tam Elbrun in _Tin Man_?

21 Why does the expert doctor in _Silicon Avatar_ destroy the Crystalline Enitity?

22 Who is Data's pen pal?

23 Why was Briam chosen to chaperone _The Perfect Mate_?

24 What does Kevin Uxbridge do in a fit of pique?

25 Why does Vash become irritated by Picard in _Q-Pid_?

26 Where did Vash and Q meet?

27 What is 'The Resolution' to Timicin in _Half A Life_?

28 What is the Borg Hugh's designation?

29 How did DaiMon Bok escape from prison?

30 What is the name of Tasha Yar's sister?

31 Who was Lwaxana's previous valet?

32 Why was he sacked?

ADMIRAL

33 What is the name of the entity which captures the Enterprise in _Where Silence Has Lease_?

34 Who rules _Angel One_?

35 Which planet does the Traveler come from?

36 What is the name of the expert doctor in _Silicon Avatar_?

37 Who is Picard's old flame in *We'll Always Have Paris*?

38 What first-contact disaster was Tam Elbrun involved in?

39 How does Worf's Klingon brother make his mark on the Enterprise crew in *Sins Of The Father*?

40 What is Ethan's real name in *Future Imperfect*?

41 Yuta is seeded with a deadly virus in *The Vengeance Factor*. What is her job?

42 What was the name of the single survivor of the Vico in *Hero Worship*?

43 Who is his hero?

44 Why does he lie about alien attackers?

45 Who was Jono in *Suddenly Human*?

46 How does he think he can resolve the agony of his decision?

47 What was the name of the amoral collector who kidnapped Data in *The Most Toys*?

48 What is the name of the girl who is actually a Q in *True Q*?

49 How does she save Riker's life?

50 What was the name of the captain of the pirate ship in *Gambit*?

51 What sensations are the Lyaarans' ambassadors intent on experiencing in *Liaisons*?

52 Who was the admiral in *The Pegasus* who had secretly developed a Federation cloaking device?

answers page 165

ENSIGN

1 In *The Last Outpost* which race stole a Federation T-9 converter?

2 Why do the inhabitants of Aldea steal the Enterprise's children in *When The Bough Breaks*?

3 Where do the crew watch Tasha Yar's obituary?

4 How many 21st century citizens are discovered in suspended animation in *The Neutral Zone*?

5 Which episode sees the first appearance of the Romulans?

6 Who do the crew find aboard a shuttle in *Time Squared*?

7 How do the nanites eventually communicate with the crew in *Evolution*?

8 How is it possible that Tasha Yar mothered a Romulan child?

9 Why did the mediator Riva need the 'Chorus Of Three' in *Loud As A Whisper*?

10 What happened to the Ferengi who ventured into the wormhole in *The Price*?

11 Which quadrant did the wormhole lead to?

12 How do Picard and Data manage to get to Romulus in *Unification*?

13 Why has Spock 'defected' to Romulus?

14 Who do the Romulan Unificationists want to unify with?

15 What is so special about the members of *The Masterpiece Society*?

16 How does Scotty survive 75 years on the crashed Jenolan?

17 How does the crew of the Enterprise attempt to destroy the Borg in *I, Borg*?

18 What is found deep underground on Earth at the beginning of *Time's Arrow*?

19 Who does the polymorphic alien in *Aquiel* disguise itself as?

20 How many Romulan defectors are being smuggled to Federation space in *Face Of The Enemy*?

21 Which other three races take part in *The Chase*?

22 What are warp drives proved to do in *Force Of Nature*?

23 How does Worf's brother propose to move the villagers to another planet in *Homeward*?

CAPTAIN

24 What is causing the Romulans some concern in *The Neutral Zone*?

25 How many Klingons did the Enterprise find on board an ancient ship in *Heart Of Glory*?

26 What does Professor Stubbs do to anger the nanites in *Evolution*?

27 What information does Admiral Jarok defect with in *The Defector*?

28 What happens to Riva's interpreters?

29 How does Riva propose to engender peace even though he is deaf and dumb?

30 Which Enterprise do the crew encounter in *Yesterday's Enterprise*?

31 Why does the Enterprise have to tow an ancient space vessel away from a planet in *Final Mission*?

32 What is the guardian protecting in the cave in *Final Mission*?

33 Why do the Ferengi kidnap Luxwana Troi in *Ménage A Troi*?

34 Why did the Ferengi want to capture the U.S.S. Hathaway in *Peak Performance*?

35 In *A Matter Of Perspective*, who actually killed Dr. Nel Apgar and destroyed the station?

36 How was Lt. Maria Aster, mother of Jeremy, killed in *The Bonding*?

37 How did the aliens responsible try to 'make it up' to Jeremy?

38 In *The Vengeance Factor*, how does Yuta plan to kill the opposing clan leader?

39 What, rather unnecessarily, does Riker do to stop her?

40 The dead crew of the U.S.S. Brittain in *Night Terrors* all had a unique chemical imbalance in their brains caused by what?

41 Symbolically, why was *The Perfect Mate* being offered as a peace gift?

42 What did the Enterprise crew find on a damaged Talarian ship in *Suddenly Human*?

43 In *Cause And Effect*, which number is transmitted into the future to remind Data?

44 What does the number represent?

45 What signal does the Enterprise transmit in order to defeat the Borg in *The Best Of Both Worlds*?

46 Why were select members of the U.S.S. Victory's crew – including Mr. La Forge – compelled to return to Tarchannen III in *Identity Crisis*?

47 How does Jellico plan to get the psychological upper hand in negotiations with the Cardassians in *Chain Of Command*?

48 What are the terrorists in *Starship Mine* after?

49 How does Gowron finally expose the Kahless imposter in *Rightful Heir*?

50 Who else is interested in *The Pegasus*?

51 How does Vorin, the Boralian escapee from the holodeck, deal with his encounter on the Enterprise in *Homeward*?

ADMIRAL

52 What do the Ligonians possess that the Federation needs so badly in *Code Of Honor*?

53 Who is leader of the conspiracy in *Conspiracy*?

54 Three 21st century citizens were recovered from cryogenic suspension onboard the U.S.S. Charleston in *The Neutral Zone*. What were their professions?

55 Which addictive drug features in *Symbiosis*?

56 Where does Pulaski examine a boy potentially infected with an ageing virus to avoid contaminating the crew in *Unnatural Selection*?

57 What event sparks off *The Drumhead* investigation?

58 How did the Klingon J'Ddan manage to smuggle Enterprise schematics off the Enterprise in *The Drumhead*?

59 How does Ral gain the upper hand in the negotiations in *The Price*?

60 How long had the Klingons been in suspended animation in *The Emissary*?

61 What was the danger in waking them up?

62 What is the technical term for *The Perfect Mate*?

63 What threatens *The Masterpiece Society*?

64 Why did the Malcorian leader Chancellor Durken refuse the Federation's *First Contact*?

65 What do the aliens need in *Night Terrors* to escape?

66 In *Reunion*, where is the bomb meant for K'Mpec concealed?

67 Which maverick Starfleet vessel is attacking Cardassians in *The Wounded*?

68 In *Data's Day*, Vulcan Ambassador T'Pel turns out to be a what?

69 What are the Cardassians suspected of developing in *Chain Of Command*?

70 Why do the androgynous J'naii asks for the Enterprise's help?

71 Who is the imposter when Picard and three other aliens are transported to a cell in *Allegiance*?

72 How does Picard expose the impostor?

73 Why does Troi's co-conspirator in *Face Of The Enemy* destroy a cargo ship?

74 How do Picard and Beverly end up on the Pyritt base in *Attached*?

75 How did Bok manage to create Picard's son in *Bloodlines*?

CAPTAIN JEAN-LUC PICARD: PERSONAL LOG

answers page 166

ENSIGN

1 What is Picard's favourite beverage?

2 Which regularly appearing Star Fleet admiral is Picard at pains to get on with in *Journey's End*?

3 What was Picard's first command ship?

4 What exactly is the Picard Maneuver?

5 What detective does Picard play on the holodeck?

6 Picard's detective exploits on the holodeck are set in which US town?

7 Is Picard left- or right-handed?

8 Name Picard's long-term Ferengi enemy.

9 What does he force Picard to do in *The Battle*?

10 In *Samaritan Snare*, what essential operation does Picard undergo?

11 Who is Picard's 'father' in *Rascals*?

12 What name did the Borg give Picard when they assimilated him?

13 How many lights does Picard see at the end of *Chain Of Command*?

14 What does Picard give Scotty as a present?

15 Why did Picard return to the Enterprise in *Starship Mine*?

16 What was the hobby of Jason Vigo, Picard's 'son'?

CAPTAIN

17 What happened when Picard first applied to SFA?

18 How come he managed to get in then?

19 How does Picard end up with an artificial heart?

20 In which episode do we see this happen?

21 Why did Picard and Jenice Manheim recreate a Parisian cafe in *We'll Always Have Paris*?

22 What is Picard suffering from at the beginning of *The Battle*?

23 Why does Picard finally acquiesce to a vacation in *Captain's Holiday*?

24 On Risa in *Captain's Holiday*, Picard buys a horgh'an. What does this statue signify?

25 What does Picard do with the Tox Uthat once he gains possession of it?

26 What watery job is Picard offered in *The Family*?

27 How does Picard square things with his brother in *The Family*?

28 Why is Picard unable to help the alien captain when the creature attacks in *Darmok*?

29 Why is Picard replaced by a doppelganger in *Allegiance*?

30 In which episode do we see Picard using a crossbow?

31 In which episode do we see Picard using a bow and arrow?

32 Why does Picard grieve when Eline dies in *The Inner Light*?

33 How does Picard, stranded in the 19th century, pass a vital message onto the 24th century crew?

34 Why does Picard die in *Tapestry*?

35 What does Picard's new love do in *Lessons* to avoid any further complications?

ADMIRAL

36 Where was Picard born?

37 What initials did Picard carve into a tree at SFA?

38 What subject did Picard fail because of that person?

39 Which athletic accolade did Picard achieve at SFA?

40 A dispute over which game resulted in Picard's post-SFA stabbing?

41 Who was Picard's weapons officer on the Stargazer?

42 Who does Picard see when the Enterprise enters a time/space distortion in *Where No One Has Gone Before*?

43 Why did Picard cunningly choose the Grisella to mediate over the colonial dispute with the Sheliak in *Ensigns Of Command*?

44 What job was Picard offered in *Coming Of Age*?

45 How does Picard disprove his perceived God-like status in *Who Watches The Watchers*?

46 What injury does Picard incur in *Disaster*?

47 What did Jono stab Picard with in *Suddenly Human*?

48 What Dickens story was Picard exploring in *Devil's Due*?

49 Who is Picard's fencing partner in *I, Borg*?

50 In *Allegiance*, a distinctly uninhibited Picard buys everyone a drink in Ten-Forward and then…?

51 What is Picard's name in *Inner Light*?

52 What is his profession?

53 Who is Picard's Cardassian interrogator in *Chain Of Command*?

54 Which member of his family does he bring into his office?

55 Which rank does Picard reach with Q's help in *Tapestry*?

56 Who did Picard fall in love with in *Lessons*?

57 What has happened to Picard in the future in *All Good Things*?

FIRST OFFICER RIKER: PERSONAL LOG

answers page 167

ENSIGN
1 What is Riker's middle name?

2 Where does Riker find his ideal love?

3 What was the setting?

4 How did Riker's father always beat him at anbo-jytsu?

5 What is the last thing Riker does to Data in the stand in *The Measure Of A Man*?

6 In *The Game*, Riker brings the game back from where?

7 How many years have seemingly passed for Riker in *Future Imperfect*?

8 What alerts Riker to the illusion in *Future Imperfect*?

9 What did Lt. Comm. Shelby want from Riker in *Best Of Both Worlds*?

10 What costume does Riker wear when the crew travel back in time in *Time's Arrow*?

CAPTAIN

11 What was Riker's first ship?

12 What is the name of Riker's father?

13 Which member of the crew has Riker's father had a relationship with?

14 What presents did Riker try to give his crewmates when he was given Q-like powers in *Hide And Q*?

15 In *Conspiracy*, what disgusting dish does Riker sample?

16 In which episode does Riker first sport his smashing new beard?

17 How do Riker and his father settle their differences?

18 In *A Matter Of Perspective*, Riker is accused of what?

19 How does Riker gain the respect of his Klingon exchange crew in *A Matter Of Honour*?

20 What does the Klingon captain do to Riker to regain his honour?

21 What game did Riker beat Ferengi Nibor at in *Ménage A Troi*?

22 What is the name of Riker's 'wife' in *Future Imperfect*?

23 What does Riker call his 'son' in *Future Imperfect*?

24 What part of Riker's anatomy is removed and then replaced overnight in *Schisms*?

25 What name did the duplicate of Riker in *Second Chances* take?

26 When the two Rikers played poker – who won?

27 What crime has Riker been institutionalised for in *Frame Of Mind*?

28 In *Parallels*, one of the alternate Enterprises was captained by a dishevelled and distraught Riker. What had happened in that universe?

ADMIRAL
29 Who captained Riker's first ship?

30 Where was Riker born?

31 Riker turns down the command of how many ships?

32 Name them.

33 Who is Riker attracted to in *Silicon Avatar*?

34 Name the Klingon ship Riker served as exchange first officer on.

35 Why does Riker have to prosecute Data in *The Measure Of A Man*?

36 What does Riker use to access engineering computers in *Disaster*?

37 Why does Riker end up in hospital in *First Contact*?

38 What two technological artefacts do the suspicious Malconians find on Riker in *First Contact*?

39 What is the name of the J'naii Riker falls in love with?

40 What ship was Riker stationed on when a freak transporter accident created a duplicate version of him?

41 What does Riker have in his hair in Data's dream in *Phantasms*?

LT. COMMANDER DATA: PERSONAL LOG

answers page 167

ENSIGN

1 Which scientist created Data?

2 Is Data left- or right-handed?

3 What colour are Data's eyes?

4 Who is Data's best friend?

5 Where is Data's 'off switch'?

6 What sort of chips make up Data's brain?

7 Who is the only person Data has slept with?

8 What is Dr. Pulaski's initial reaction to Data?

9 What was the name of Data's classic poem?

10 What is the name of Data's brother?

11 Who is the only person Data has used the Vulcan death grip on?

12 What is the name of Data's cat?

13 What colour is it?

14 What sex is it?

15 Why does Data's creator summon him to a far-off planet in *Brothers*?

16 What does Lore steal from Data in *Brothers*?

17 Who gives Data the gift of a really good laugh?

18 How does Data cure the crew of *The Game*'s addiction?

19 How does Data raise money in 19th century San Francisco?

20 In which episode does Data experience his first emotion?

21 What is Data's first emotion?

22 What does Data's mother turn out to be in *Inheritance*?

23 Does Data tell his mother?

CAPTAIN

24 Which planet was Data originally found on?

25 What did Data do before he was given a modesty program?

26 How many women has Data had 'relationships' with?

27 On his official record, Data is listed as 'Lt. Cmdr. NFN NMI Data'. What do the abbreviations mean?

28 What is Data's actual job on the ship?

29 In which episode does Data 'grow' a beard?

30 In *The Outrageous Okona* Data performs what?

31 Who is described as Data's grandfather in *The Schizoid Man*?

32 What two things are described by Data as being 'intimate' to him in *The Measure Of A Man*?

33 What was Data's daughter called?

34 What language does her name come from?

35 And what does it mean?

36 How was Data's daughter an 'improvement' over Data himself?

37 Which crew member does Data's daughter kiss in _The Offspring_?

38 How does Fajo get Data to capitulate to his demands in _The Most Toys_?

39 Why does Data disobey a direct order in _Clues_?

40 Who, on Data's ship in _Redemption II_, decides to resign?

41 Why?

42 How many characters does Data play in _A Fistful Of Datas_?

43 Who?

44 Why does Data turn off his chronometer in _Timescape_?

45 What observation of Data's saves the ship in _Genesis_?

46 In which episode does Data stab Troi with a knife?

ADMIRAL

47 How many androids did Data's 'father' make before Data?

48 What was the name of Data's 'mother'?

49 How much does Data weigh (in kg)?

50 Data has been seen to feed his cat with feline supplement number…?

51 In which episode does Data sing?

52 In which episode does Data try to grasp the rudiments of comedy?

53 As of the first episode of TNG, how long has Data been in Starfleet?

54 Which Data is the 'real' Data when time distortions in *We'll Always Have Paris* split him into three?

55 How long has Data to convince the colonists of a Sheliak planet to leave in *Ensigns Of Command*?

56 In which episode does Data attack and hurt both La Forge and Picard?

57 What game does Data lose in *Peak Performance*?

58 What shape does Data think he can see in the nebula in *Imaginary Friend*?

59 How does Data first plan to avoid being the object under Bruce Maddox's laser scalpel?

60 Who does Data believe he is when the crew lose their memories in *Conundrum*?

61 Why?

62 What does Rasmussen, in *A Matter Of Time*, call Data?

63 What job does Data's daughter get on the Enterprise?

64 What ship does Data command in *Redemption Part II*?

65 What did Security Officer Jenna D'Sora, Data's girlfriend in *In Theory*, give him as a present?

66 What accident caused Data's first dream?

67 What profession did Dr. Soong seem to be in Data's dream in *Birthright*?

68 In *Descent*, what other emotion does Data feel after killing the Borg?

69 And who would he kill to feel emotions again?

70 Data has the logs of how many colonists in his data banks?

71 What does Data find inside his chest in *Phantasms*?

72 In *Phantasms*, what is Data's subconscious imagery actually pointing to?

73 In *Phantasms*, what does Data do to hurt the miners?

74 Which character from which play is Data playing at the beginning of *Emergence*?

LIEUTENANT WORF: PERSONAL LOG

answers page 168

ENSIGN

1 Who is Worf's cute but annoying son?

2 Where does Worf exercise?

3 Who was Worf's beloved?

4 What rank did she hold?

5 How does she arrive on the Enterprise?

6 Who killed her?

7 What is Worf's Klingon brother called?

8 Why does Worf suffer discommendation?

9 In *The Enemy*, Worf is asked to give what to save a Romulan's life?

10 And does he?

11 What injury does Worf sustain in *Ethics*?

12 How?

13 How do the crew ensure Worf celebrates the tenth anniversary of his Rite of Ascension?

14 Who does Worf think he should check with before 'dating' Troi?

15 Who is K'mtar in *Firstborn*?

CAPTAIN
16 Who is Nikolai Roshenko?

17 What was the name of Worf's father?

18 Where did he die?

19 Who calls Worf 'handsome' in *The Emissary*?

20 Which dish, cooked by Riker, does Worf love?

21 How do Worf and his brother meet for the first time?

22 Why does Worf reject Alexander's mother's advances in *Reunion*?

23 In which episode does Worf resign?

24 Who does Worf ask to care for his son should he die in *Ethics*?

25 How does Worf finally get his son to stay with him?

26 How does Worf defeat the lightning reflexes of Data in *A Fistful Of Datas*?

27 What is Worf proudly demonstrating at the beginning of *Genesis*?

28 True or false: Worf actually has an affair with Ensign Calloway in *Eye Of The Beholder*.

ADMIRAL
29 What place does Worf have in Starfleet history?

30 Kahlest is what relation to Worf?

31 How does Worf satisfy the Klingon fugitive in *Heart Of Glory*?

32 What did Worf and Dr. Pulaski share in *Up The Long Ladder*?

33 What is Riker's nickname for Worf in *The Emissary*?

34 In *Peak Performance*, what does Worf do to distract the Enterprise?

35 In which episode is Worf killed and then brought back to life?

36 How long ago (in *Emissary*) did Worf have a relationship with a Klingon Ambassador?

37 Why does Worf purposely cut his hand on a Klingon dagger in *Redemption II*?

38 What position did Worf take on Gowron's flagship in *Redemption II*?

39 In one of the parallel universes in *Parallels*, Worf is the husband of Deanna Troi. After which event in Worf's life is this 'mating' mooted to have occurred?

40 What is Worf's son caught doing in *New Ground*?

41 What is Toq gardening with in *Birthright* that so incenses Worf?

42 What does Worf do to Riker when demonstrating the effectiveness of the Tilonian nisroh blade in *Frame Of Mind*?

43 What is Worf rehearsing at the beginning of *Firstborn*?

– LT. COMMANDER GEORDI LA FORGE: PERSONAL LOG

answers page 169

ENSIGN

1 What rank has Geordi been promoted to in *The Child*?

2 What happens to Geordi in *The Mind's Eye*?

3 Who notices the difference in Geordi's behaviour?

4 What would have happened to Geordi had he been born in *The Masterpiece Society*?

5 How long has Geordi been blind?

6 Whom does Geordi see whilst piloting a virtual reality device in *Interface*?

CAPTAIN

7 How did Geordi lose his sight?

8 How many times has Geordi been offered his sight back?

9 What does Geordi complain of when he appears in sickbay over and over again in *Cause And Effect*?

10 In which episode does La Forge create the designer of the Enterprise's engines?

11 What was her name?

ADMIRAL

12 Geordi's mother was captain of which ship?

13 What does Geordi's dad do?

14 What rank does Geordi take on the U.S.S. Excalibur in *Redemption*?

15 What was Geordi's ship before the Enterprise as related in *Night Terrors*?

16 Who had a crush on Geordi in *Phantasms*?

COUNSELLOR TROI: PERSONAL LOG

answers page 169

ENSIGN

1 Who has Troi had a relationship with before she joins the Enterprise?

2 How long ago was this relationship?

3 What is the name of Troi's mother?

4 What is her butler called?

5 In which episode do we first meet her?

6 What is Troi's favourite food?

7 How does Troi pass the bridge test?

8 In which episode does Troi give birth to a fast-growing child?

9 In *The Loss*, what does Troi lose?

10 What is Troi's mother's deepest secret?

11 What did Troi start to turn into in *Genesis*?

CAPTAIN

12 What did Troi study as a student?

13 What happens to Troi in *Man Of The People*?

14 Why?

15 What role does Barclay give Troi in his holodeck fantasy?

16 What sort of cake is Troi's belly made of in *Phantasms*?

17 When Troi takes command of the bridge in *Disaster*, who else is on hand to help?

18 In *The Loss*, Troi takes what career move?

19 How does Kevin Uxbridge stop Troi from detecting him?

20 What does Captain Jellico, who takes over from Picard in *Chain Of Command*, demand of Troi?

21 What is the *Dark Page* in Lwaxana's mind?

ADMIRAL

22 What is the name of Troi's father?

23 What did Troi name her child?

24 What was the name of Troi's dead sister?

25 What is Counsellor Troi's favourite fruit?

26 How long is Troi pregnant for?

27 What is the name of the human Troi was destined to marry in *Haven*?

28 What fact does Troi's mother reveal about the Antedians in *Manhunt*?

29 What is the name of the negotiator Troi falls for in *The Price*?

30 How did Troi manage to break Worf's wrist in *Clues*?

31 What rank is Troi when she is disguised as a Romulan in *Face Of The Enemy*?

DOCTOR BEVERLY CRUSHER: PERSONAL LOG
answers page 169

ENSIGN
1 What does Beverly teach Data to do in *Data's Day*?

2 What is the name of Beverly's nurse in later episodes?

3 What scuppers Bev's relationship with Odan in *The Host*?

4 Where does the ghost which haunts the Crusher family hide in *Sub Rosa*?

5 Why does Beverly Crusher resign in *Sub Rosa*?

CAPTAIN
6 What post does Beverly Crusher take to explain her absence in the second season of TNG?

7 What was Bev's maiden name?

8 What recreational activity is Bev particularly skilled at?

9 What name does Bev give the amnesiac stranger in *Transfigurations*?

10 What happens to Beverly in *Remember Me*?

11 Who saves Beverly?

12 Why does Bev incur Picard's wrath when she performs an autopsy on the Ferengi Dr. Regar in *Suspicions*?

13 Why does Bev incur the Ferengis' wrath when she performs said autopsy on said Ferengi doctor in said episode?

ADMIRAL

14 Where was Bev born?

15 How did Bev's husband die?

16 What was Picard's role in the tragedy?

17 Who is forced to relive this event?

18 Who is Dalen Quaice?

19 Name three plays Bev has directed on board the Enterprise.

20 What was the full name of Bev's grandmother?

21 What was the name of this life form in *Sub Rosa*?

22 What was the name of Beverly's ship in *All Good Things…*?

ENSIGN WESLEY CRUSHER: PERSONAL LOG

answers page 170

ENSIGN

1 What was the name of Wesley's late father?

2 What is the name of Wesley's other-worldly mentor who appears in several episodes?

3 How does Wes do in the Academy entrance exam in *Coming Of Age*?

4 In *Family*, Wes meets who on the holodeck?

5 Which culture did Wesley choose to live with in *Journey's End*?

CAPTAIN

6 What colour uniform does Wes wear in the first series of TNG?

7 In which episode does Wesley reconfigure the ship's tractor beams as a repulsor beam?

8 In *Justice*, Wes is nearly executed for doing what?

9 How was he to be executed?

10 How old was Wes when he attempted to enter SFA?

11 Which other races are represented when Wesley takes the SFA exam?

12 In which episode does Wesley finally go the SFA?

13 But what happens en route?

14 What event is Wesley Crusher forced to experience at SFA?

15 What was the name of Wesley's flight squadron at SFA?

ADMIRAL

16 How old is Wesley at the start of the first series of TNG?

17 What rank was Wesley's father when he died?

18 Which flight manoeuvre almost causes Wesley's expulsion from Starfleet Academy?

19 Who is Wesley's girlfriend in *The Game*?

20 Who is Wesley compared to by the Traveler in *Where No One Has Gone Before*?

21 In which episode is Wesley promoted to full ensign?

ENSIGN RO: PERSONAL LOG

answers page 170

ENSIGN

1 What race is Ensign Ro?

2 What does Ro believe has happened to her in *The Next Phase*?

3 What is Ensign Ro's first name?

CAPTAIN

4 Which two physical characteristics typify Ro's race?

5 What was Ro's first bridge station on the Enterprise?

6 Which member of the crew has Ro slept with?

7 In which episode?

ADMIRAL

8 Which ship did Ro serve on before the Enterprise?

9 What happened to her in between?

10 What is Ro's plan in *Disaster*?

11 Why was Ro court-martialled?

Q: PERSONAL LOG

answers page 170

ENSIGN

1 What did Q do to a security officer to prove his power in *Encounter At Farpoint*?

2 How much time does Q give Picard to prove humanity's worth in the same episode?

3 What choices does Q give Amanda Rogers in *True Q*?

4 What did Q give to Data as a parting gift in *Deja Q*?

5 Where does Q hail from?

CAPTAIN

6 How many episodes of TNG has Q appeared in?

7 Name them.

8 When Q transports the bridge crew onto an inhospitable planet populated by nasty furry animals, which two crew members die in the subsequent battle (only to be resurrected later on)?

9 How does Q regain his powers in *Deja Q*?

ADMIRAL

10 How many pips does Q have when in a Starfleet uniform?

11 What uniform does Q wear in *Hide And Q*?

12 What is Q's name on the planet of Brax ?

13 What is Q's IQ?

14 What form did the Q take to destroy Amanda Rogers' parents?

EPISODES

answers page 170

1   In which episode does Picard draw a smiley on a warp core breach?

2   In which three episodes do we see Troi and Worf get together (sort of)?

3   In which three episodes does Troi get to captain a ship?

4   Which two episodes feature 'phased cloak' technology?

5   In which episode does Picard fall in love with Lt. Comm. Nella Daren?

6   In which episode does Riker lose his arm in the middle of the night?

7   Metaphasic shielding was used twice: in which episodes?

8   We first meet DaiMon Bok in which episode?

9   In which episode does Riker square up with his dad?

10 In which episode does Troi become a Romulan?

11 In which episode is Geordi trapped on the surface of a planet with a Romulan?

12 In which episode does Data first seem to want to take a human's life?

13 In which episode is Picard kidnapped and tortured?

14 In which three episodes does the saucer section separate from the ship?

15 In which episode is Data put on trial for his humanity?

16 When do the Ferengi give the Stargazer back to Picard?

17 In which episode do we first meet the Trill?

18 In which episode do we see Data seduced by a crew member?

19 In which episode does Picard repay the crimes of his ancestors perpetrated on the American Indians?

20 In which episode does Data meet his mother?

21 In which episode does Barclay give lessons to Einstein?

22 In which episode do Riker, Worf and some other crew members collectively recreate their own shared dream on the Holodeck?

23 In which episode does Ro infiltrate the Maquis?

24 Which episode saw K'Ehleyr's first appearance?

25 In which episode is the Yamato destroyed?

26 In which episode does an alien lifeform think the NCC-1701-D is its mother?

27 In which episode are the Borg first seen?

28 Worf has commanded the Enterprise twice. In which episodes?

29 In which episode is Data thrown back to 19th century San Francisco?

30 In which episode has Data become holder of the Lucsian chair at Cambridge University?

31 In which two episodes is Geordi offered his sight back?

32 When did Picard make a child his 'number one'?

33 In which episode does Riker serve as an exchange officer on a Klingon ship?

34 In which episode was Picard believed to be a God?

35 In which episode did Dr. Pulaski first appear?

36 In which episode is Wesley Crusher promoted to full ensign?

37 In which episode does Picard mind-meld with Spock's father?

38 In which episode is Worf discommended?

39 In which episode does Geordi 'kill' Chief O'Brien?

40 Which episode, in which the crew lose their inhibitions, 'borrows' from a CT plot?

41 In which episode is Deanna Troi forced to take part in an arranged marriage?

42 In which episode is Keiko's baby born?

43 In which episode does Guinan first appear?

44 Which episode opens with the death of Picard?

45 Which episode has the crew encountering a steadfastly matriarchal race?

46 *The Offspring* is a 'cover version' of which CT episode?

47 In which episode do the entire crew lose their memories?

48 In *The Wounded* we meet which race for the first time?

49 In which episode do we see the original CT bridge in all its tacky primary-coloured glory?

50 What was the name of the last TNG episode ever (boo-hoo, wringing of hands etc)?

DEEP SPACE

DEEP SPACE

MULTIPLE CHOICE
answers page 171

ENSIGN

1 Who is Martus caught 'consorting' with in *Rivals*?
 a) Lwaxana Troi
 b) A Dabo girl.
 c) Major Kira.

2 What is Dr. Bashir's first name?
 a) Jules
 b) Julian.
 c) Jeremy.

3 What is the common title for Bajoran holy people?
 a) Vedek.
 b) Father.
 c) Kai.

4 Which race built DS9?
 a) The Bajorans.
 b) The Cardassians.
 c) The Romulans.

CAPTAIN

5 Who teaches Nog to read?
 a) Jake Sisko
 b) Benjamin Sisko.
 c) Quark.

6 In *Blood Oath*, what is the name of the Klingon's arch enemy?
 a) The Romulan.
 b) The Skull.
 c) The Albino

7 Who runs Deep Space Nine in the mirror universe?
 a) Sisko.
 b) Kira.

c) Dax.

8 Approximately how old is Dax?
a) 600 years.
b) 750 years.
c) 400 years.

ADMIRAL

9 How do Odo and Croden destroy Ah-Kel's ship in *Vortex*?
a) By tempting him to fire within a flammable nebula.
b) By using the Runabout's phasers.
c) By transporting over and activating the ship's self-destruct.

10 In which episode are the parents of an adopted Cardassian boy accused of mistreating their son?
a) *Cardassians*.
b) *The Adopted*.
c) *The Forsaken*.

11 At what age did Kira start fighting the Cardassians?
a) Nine.
b) Twelve.
c) Fourteen.

12 What is the first Rule of Acquisition?
a) You're only as good as your last deal.
b) Profit above everything.
c) Once you have the money, never give it back.

CREW

answers page 171

ENSIGN

1 Whose mind does the alien in *The Passenger* occupy?

2 Who unwillingly becomes *The Storyteller*?

3 Which four members of the crew were drawn into the *Move Along Home* game?

4 Who was 'killed' first during the game?

5 Whose wishes bring a baseball player to life in *If Wishes Were Horses*?

6 In *Whispers*, who is under suspicion by the rest of the crew?

7 In *The Homecoming* who decides to rescue a mythical Bajoran leader?

CAPTAIN

8 What do Sisko, Dr. Bashir, Dax, and Kira initially think they are sharing in *Move Along Home*?

9 Who almost started another war between Bajora and Cardassia in *The Homecoming*?

10 How?

11 Which DS9 officers discovered the first stable wormhole in the known universe?

12 What sides are the crew compelled to take when the station is overcome by an ancient alien virus in *Dramatis Personae*?

13 Which character is absent from the parallel universe in *Crossover*?

14 Which crew members travelled with the Kai through the wormhole to the Gamma Quadrant?

15 What abilities does Sisko's and Quark's fellow prisoner have in *The Jem'hadar*?

16 Who helps Kira do what she has to in *The Homecoming*?

ADMIRAL

17 Why are Bashir and O'Brien attacked after helping a race destroy their deadly bioweapons?

18 How do Sisko, Dr. Bashir, Dax and Kira get past the third 'shap'?

19 Who remains unaffected by the virus in *Dramatis Personae*, and – inevitably – saves the day?

20 What ancient schoolyard game do the crew have to play to move along another 'shap' in *Move Along Home*?

21 Why did the crew initially believe Marritza was Gul Darhe'el in *Duet*?

22 What is the nature of the object Dax and the Trill initiate bring back home from the Gamma Quadrant in *Playing God*?

CHARACTERS
answers page 171

ENSIGN
1 Who runs the bar on DS9?

2 What is the name of the only Cardassian left on board DS9?

3 What is his profession?

4 What 'apparently' happens to the Royal Nagus Zek in *The Nagus*?

5 How did Vash end up in the Gamma Quadrant?

6 Which Kai died in *Battle Lines* and what happens to her?

7 Whose teachings did Vedek Winn objects to in *In The Hands Of The Prophets*?

8 Why is Melora confined to a wheelchair?

CAPTAIN
9 Who was the first visitor from the Gamma Quadrant?

10 What is the name of the walrus-like alien who haunts the bar on DS9?

11 Who does Lwaxana Troi set her sights on in *The Forsaken*?

12 What was the name of the virus which infected DS9's computer systems in *The Forsaken*?

13 What are Lursa and B'Etor doing in the environs of DS9 in *Past Prologue*?

14 Who organised the assassination attempt on Vedek Bareil in *In The Hands Of The Prophets*?

15 What did Marritza, who pretended to be a 'famed Cardassian war tyrant', do when he heard screaming Bajorans being slaughtered?

16 Who are Kor, Koloth, and Kang?

ADMIRAL

17 Why did Ro-Kel vow to kill Croden in *Vortex*?

18 How much does Q finally bid at the auction in *Q-Less*?

19 What position did Anara, the Bajoran assassin, hold on DS9 in *The Forsaken*?

20 How does Marritza die in *Duet*?

21 What was the name of the intransigent Bajoran father in *Progress*?

22 What was the name of the jealous Trill in *Invasive Procedures*?

23 What was the name of the alien fugitive O'Brien befriended in *Captive Pursuit*?

24 What was the meaning of his existence?

25 What do Nog and Jake trade yamok sauce for in *Progress*?

26 What do they then go on to trade them for?

27 Who is found to be leader of *The Maquis*?

answers page 172

ENSIGN

1   What are the first symptoms of the aphasia virus in *Babel*?

2   What creates the Dal'Rok in *The Storyteller*?

3   Who is suspected of being a collaborator in *The Collaborator*?

4   Who became Kai of Bajor in *The Collaborator*?

5   What is the name of the Bajoran anti-government organisation which threatens the station at the end of the first season of DS9?

6   In *Invasive Procedures*, what do the invaders want?

7   In *Sanctuary*, what planet do the refugees believe is 'the promised land'?

8   In *Paradise*, what have the stranded Starfleet crew lived without?

CAPTAIN

9   What causes the runabout to crash-land on a moon in the Gamma Quadrant in *Battle Lines*?

10   Where was the aphasia virus located in *Babel*?

11   Who planted the virus on DS9?

12   What did Croden have stashed away in a stasis chamber in an asteroid belt in *Vortex*?

13   Where is Ibudan murdered in *A Man Alone*?

14   How come Ibudan wasn't actually murdered?

15   What does Vash's artefact end up being in *Q-Less*?

ADMIRAL

16 In *Past Prologue*, Tahna intends to do what with the explosives he buys?

17 Why?

18 What does *The Passenger* want to steal?

19 What was stolen from Lwaxana Troi in *The Forsaken*?

20 Where on DS9 does Lwaxanna intend to picnic the hapless Odo?

21 On board which type of vessel does Odo leave Croden?

22 How does Neela manage to get a weapon on the promenade in *In The Hands Of The Prophets*?

POT POURRI

answers page 172

ENSIGN

1 In the opening sequence, what draws attention to DS9?

2 If the Gamma Quadrant is 7000 light years from Federation space how does one get there?

3 What is a symbiont?

4 What is the name of the shadowy organisation in the Gamma Quadrant?

5 Who are the even shadowier group which founded it?

6 And who are their warriors?

CAPTAIN

7 Which two characters have guest starred in TNG and DS9?

8 What do the entities who live in the wormhole not understand about human existence?

9 What is the name of Starfleet best battleship in *The Search*?

10 Why is it so heavily armed?

ADMIRAL
11 What sorts of readings precede a ship coming through the wormhole?

12 Which baseball player beat Joe DiMaggio's record for consecutive hits?

13 What is the aim of the Altonian Brain Teaser?

COMMANDER SISKO: PERSONAL LOG
answers page 172

ENSIGN
1 What is Sisko's first name?

2 What is Sisko's son called?

3 What is Sisko's favourite sport?

4 Has Sisko ever set foot on the Enterprise?

5 What title do the Bajoran monks give Sisko?

CAPTAIN
6 How did Sisko lose his wife?

7 What was the name of Sisko's wife?

8 What is Q's nickname for Sisko?

9 In *Crossover*, what type of character is the alternate Sisko?

ADMIRAL
10 How many years after losing his wife did Sisko take command of DS9?

11 What starship did Sisko serve on?

12 Where did Sisko work before he came to DS9?

13 How does Sisko convince Quark to stay on DS9 in *Emissary*?

14 What is Sisko's favourite dish?

MAJOR KIRA: PERSONAL LOG

answers page 172

ENSIGN

1 Kira meets Tahna in *Past Prologue*. Whom did they both once work for?

2 What does Kira pretend to be on the Cardassian prison planet in *The Homecoming*?

3 Who does Kira have a relationship with?

CAPTAIN

4 What is Kira's ambassadorial function on DS9?

5 In which episode does Major Kira have an 'orb-experience'?

6 In which episode is Major Kira replaced?

7 How does Kira get the stubborn farmer Mullibok to move in *Progress*?

8 What sacrifice does Major Kira temporarily make to help Mullibok?

ADMIRAL

9 Which legendary Bajoran war hero does Kira believe should be leader of the Bajorans?

10 What description of Kira by the Cardassians incensed her so much?

LIEUTENANT DAX: PERSONAL LOG

answers page 172

ENSIGN

1 What race is Dax?

2 Which member of the DS9 crew knew Dax in a previous 'incarnation'?

3 What is Sisko's informal nickname for Dax?

4 What was Dax's first name before Jadzia?

CAPTAIN

5 What happens to Dax in *Invasive Procedures*?

6 Why could Dax not have committed the crime he/she is accused of in *Dax*?

ADMIRAL

7 When was Dax last a female?

8 How many times has Dax been a mother?

9 And a father?

10 Who is Dax accused of murdering in *Dax*?

11 How long can a Trill symbiont survive without its host?

12 How long has Dax been trying to master the Altonian Brain Teaser?

CHIEF O'BRIEN: PERSONAL LOG

answers page 173

ENSIGN

1   What are Chief O'Brien's first names?

2   Who gave Keiko away at O'Brien and Keiko's wedding?

3   What race does O'Brien have a deep prejudice against?

4   Where were Keiko and O'Brien married?

5   Where is O'Brien going when he is arrested by the Cardassians in *Tribunal*?

CAPTAIN

6   What is the name of the Chief's and Keiko's child?

7   What does O'Brien's daughter conjure up in *If Wishes Were Horses*?

8   Who helped Keiko give birth?

9   What is O'Brien's nickname for the Cardassians?

10 What do the Cardassians remove from O'Brien in *Tribunal*?

ADMIRAL

11 Which is Chief O'Brien's favourite transporter room?

12 How many brothers does O'Brien have?

13 Who tries to kill O'Brien in *The Storyteller*?

14 What is O'Brien mortally afraid of?

ODO: PERSONAL LOG

answers page 173

ENSIGN

1 Where does Odo retire when he reverts to liquid?

2 Why does Odo look 'not quite' human?

3 Who is the only person to have seen Odo return to his original form?

4 What is Odo's official rank?

CAPTAIN

5 How often does Odo have to revert to liquid form?

6 What does the alien fugitive in *Vortex* give to Odo to prove his knowledge that other shape-shifters exist?

7 When he was first found, Odo used to do what to 'fit in'?

8 What connection does Dr. Mora Pol have to Odo?

9 What role does the alternate-Odo have in running the station?

ADMIRAL

10 Where was Odo found?

11 Why does the murder of Ibudan in *A Man Alone* implicate Odo in particular?

12 How do the bad guys in *Invasive Procedures* disable Odo?

13 In which episode does Odo feel threatened by a recently recruited Starfleet security officer?

QUARK: PERSONAL LOG

answers page 173

ENSIGN

1 What is the name of Quark's brother?

2 Quark's nephew, friend of Sisko's son, is called?

3 What's the roulette type game played in Quark's bar?

CAPTAIN

4 Why do the aliens from the Gamma Quadrant force Quark to play *Move Along Home*?

5 How come Quark doesn't manage to get a seat on the ships evacuating DS9 in *The Siege*?

6 What reward does Quark give his brother for attempting to throw him out of the airlock?

7 What does Quark find behind the wall in *Necessary Evil*?

ADMIRAL

8 Name Quark's cousin?

9 What did Quark do to him?

10 Whom did Krax, the Grand Nagus's son, plot with to kill Quark in *The Nagus*?

11 What was the name of the game Quark was forced to play in *Move Along Home*?

BAJORAN CULTURE AND HISTORY

answers page 173

ENSIGN

1 What is your 'pagh'?

2   What is the title of the Bajoran religious leader?

3   Who are 'The Circle'?

CAPTAIN
4   What do the orthodox religious leaders of Bajor call the wormhole?

5   And who lives there apparently?

6   How many Orbs were originally in Bajoran possession?

7   Who now owns the majority of the Orbs?

8   For how many thousands of years have the Bajorans been studying the Orbs?

9   What was the Bajoran 'Higa Metor'?

ADMIRAL
10 What is the biggest Bajoran holiday of the year?

11 What are 'pulukus'?

12 How long was the Cardassian's occupation of Bajora?

13 Who was the leader of '*The Circle*'?

FERENGI CULTURE AND HISTORY
answers page 173

ENSIGN
1   Which rules govern a Ferengi's life?

2   Who is the leader of the Ferengi?

3   What do Ferengi women wear?

4   Where are a Ferengi's erogenous zones?

CAPTAIN

5 Who is the current Grand Nagus of the Ferengi?

6 The ninth rule of Acquisition reads: 'Opportunity + instinct ='
what?

7 The sixth rule of Acquisition reads: 'Never let _____ stand in the
way of opportunity'. Fill in the blank.

8 A Ferengi captain is called a...?

ADMIRAL

9 How many rules of Acquisition are there?

10 The 31st rule of Acquisition reads: 'Never make fun of a Ferengi's
_____'. Fill in the blank.

11 The 21st rule of Acquisition reads: 'Never place _____ over
profit.' Fill in the blank.

12 What does the hammer symbolise for the Ferengi?

13 What would you do to a Ferengi when taking part in 'oo-mox'?

CARDASSIAN CULTURE AND HISTORY

answers page 173

ENSIGN

1 What is the prefix of a high ranking military Cardassian's name?

2 Which Cardassian military official was the last prefect of Bajor?

CAPTAIN

3 Who was the infamous Gul Darhe'el?

4 How are all defendants in a Cardassian court found?

ADMIRAL

5 What was the Cardassian name for DS9?

6 What is a Cardassian likely to do with a Kamar?

— DEEP SPACE NINE HISTORY AND SPECIFICATIONS

answers page 174

ENSIGN

1 Most amenities on DS9 are centred around a central hub called...?

2 What shape are the computer screens on DS9?

3 Who runs the school on DS9?

4 What is the bartering currency on DS9?

5 What are Quark's adult entertainment areas called?

CAPTAIN

6 What is the difference between TNG and DS9 Starfleet uniforms?

7 On the Enterprise it's the bridge, on DS9, however, it's...?

8 Name the three DS9 runabouts.

9 What areas are to be found on DS9's habitat ring?

10 What is the sickbay on DS9 called?

ADMIRAL

11 How old was DS9 when the Cardassians relinquished possession of it?

12 How many people can DS9 accommodate at maximum capacity?

13 What is the usual crew complement on DS9?

14 The Enterprise uses isolinear chips, what does DS9 use?

15 Why was DS9 in such a state when the Federation moved in?

EPISODES

answers page 174

1 What was the name of the first feature-length episode of DS9?

2 In which episode does the Kai traverse the wormhole?

3 Which episode sees Vash and Q visit DS9?

4 In which episode is Dax on trial for murder?

5 In which episode do we see an alternate universe first encountered by Captain Kirk?

6 In which episode is Odo assaulted by a crowd of misled bigots?

7 A Bajoran village is threatened by the Dal'Rok in which episode?

8 In which episode does the ruler of the Ferengi Empire make an appearance?

9 In which episode is Dax compelled to fulfil an oath she made to a trio of Klingons?

10 In which episode do we first see a Ferengi female?

11 Which three episodes made up the first ever three-part story in Trek history?

12 In which episode do the Duras sisters appear?

13 In which episode do we first meet the station's tailor?

14 In which episode does Odo find the first clue to his origins?

THE FILMS

THE FILMS

I: THE MOTION PICTURE

answers page 174

1 What rank is Kirk in ST I?

2 Who is a "chairbound paperpusher' at the start of the film?

3 Who was the Enterprise Captain before Kirk boards?

4 Decker is the son of captain Matthew Decker. In which CT episode did we see him die?

5 What rank has Chekov attained in this film?

6 What is V'ger searching for?

7 What does V'ger call humans?

8 What peril does the Enterprise face during its first leap into warp space?

9 Why does Spock rejoin the Enterprise from Vulcan?

10 How does Spock communicate with the probe?

11 What is the name of the bald woman who is absorbed by V'ger?

12 What command post does she hold?

13 What is V'ger revealed as being?

14 What happens to Decker?

II: THE WRATH OF KHAN

answers page 174

1   How old is Kirk at the start of this film?

2   What presents does he receive for his birthday?

3   Which original crew members are present in the opening scene?

4   What is the 'Kobayashi Maru'?

5   Who is the only cadet to have ever beaten it?

6   How?

7   What race is Saavik?

8   What was the name of Khan's Ship?

9   What is Khan's full name?

10   What was the name of Khan's wife?

11   What position did she hold on the CT Enterprise?

12   How did she die?

13   Why is Ceti Alpha V no longer the lush paradise it was?

14   Which Starfleet vessel, staffed by Chekov, does Khan steal?

15   What is the name of the research station in ST II?

16   Who invented the Genesis device?

17   How does Kirk know her?

18   What is the name of Kirk's son?

19   It took three months to carve out the cave in the moon, but it took Genesis how long to produce the lush vegetation?

20   How does Captain Terrell avoid killing Kirk?

21 How does Kirk lower Khan's ship's shields?

22 What coded phrase does Kirk use when speaking to Spock to disguise his intent?

23 What does Khan wear as a necklace?

24 Approximately how old was Khan when he died?

25 How exactly does Spock save the ship?

26 What is the name of the nebula from which the Genesis planet is formed?

27 Who dies at the end of the film?

28 What acts as his coffin?

III: THE SEARCH FOR SPOCK

answers page 175

1 Who believes, initially, that Kirk is host to Spock's spirit?

2 What did Spock do to McCoy?

3 How does Kirk ascertain that Spock has done something to McCoy?

4 What do the crew do when they are refused permission to take the Enterprise.

5 What is so special about the Excelsior's propulsion system?

6 What is the Excelsior's registration number?

7 Why doesn't the Excelsior intercept the Enterprise?

8 What is the name of the Klingon commander who wants the Genesis Project?

9 Which Starfleet vessels is in orbit around the Genesis planet?

10 Why can't the Enterprise engage the Klingon ship?

11 How does Kirk's son die?

12 What does Kirk do the Enterprise at the end of the film?

13 What is the name of the Vulcan priestess who attempts the fal-tor-pan?

14 Who performs the ceremony to put Spock's spirit back into Spock?

15 Whom does Spock first recognise after being reunited with his mind?

16 What happens to the Genesis planet?

IV: THE VOYAGE HOME

answers page 175

1 Who defends Kirk in front of the Federation Council?

2 What do the crew rechristen the Klingon bird of prey?

3 How many computers is Spock simultaneously operating during his rehabiliation session?

4 Which question completely flummoxes Spock when asked by the computer?

5 Who stays behind on Vulcan?

6 How is the alien probe gradually destroying the Earth?

7 What is the exact breed of whale the alien probe wishes to communicate with?

8 How does the Enterprise manage to travel back in time?

9 Which CT episode first featured exactly the same time travel method?

10 Which city does the crew land in?

11 Who sees them land?

12 What does Spock do to conceal his 'Vulcan-ness'?

13 Who does Spock render unconscious on the bus?

14 Why?

15 What is the name of marine biologist who falls for Kirk?

16 What are the names of the two whales?

17 How does Spock know one of the whales is pregnant?

18 What 20th century method of transport does Sulu pilot?

19 Which two crew members are sent to the Enterprise aircraft carrier?

20 Why are the whales released a day early?

21 Who is captured by the navy?

22 What is the method the crew use to recrystallize the dilithium crystals?

23 How do they get the whales on board the bird of prey?

24 How does Spock account for the mass of the whales in his calculations for the return trip through time?

25 How many Starfleet regulations violations is Kirk charged with?

26 What is Kirk's punishment for his crimes in ST III?

V: THE FINAL FRONTIER

answers page 175

1   Where do we find our favourite crew members camping at the start of the film?

2   What is the auspicious title of the planet Nimbus III?

3   What is the capital of Nimbus III?

4   Which three races live in 'harmony' there?

5   What relation is Spock to Sybok?

6   What is Sybok's quest?

7   Which two methods does Sybok use to convert people to his cause?

8   Which fear must McCoy face?

9   Why does Bones blame himself for this incident?

10 Which experience must Spock relive?

11 Why does Kirk resist Sybok?

12 What normally prevents ships from penetrating the centre of the galaxy?

13 What is the name of the shuttle craft the crew pilot down to 'God's planet'?

14 What does 'God' request of the crew?

15 What form does 'God' take to attack Sybok?

16 What song do Spock, Kirk, and Bones sing at the end of ST V?

VI: THE UNDISCOVERED COUNTRY

answers page 175

1   What is the Undiscovered Country?

2   What moon is the key energy source for the Klingon empire?

3   What ship does Sulu captain?

4   How many years to live is the Klingon Empire given after the destruction of their energy source?

5   Why does Kirk hate the Klingons so much?

6   Who is the leader of the Klingon High Council at the time of ST VI?

7   What was the name of Christopher Plummer's character in the film?

8   What was the name of the Klingon Ambassador's ship apparently fired on by the by the Enterprise?

9   Which new prototype Klingon vessel is shown in ST VI?

10 How many 'hit men' transported over to the Klingon ship?

11 What crime do Kirk and McCoy stand trial for?

12 What is the name of the Klingons' penal asteroid?

13 What is a cameloid?

14 What is the name of the shapeshifter Kirk befriends?

15 Who was Gorkon succeeded by?

16 How did Spock expose Valeris's guilt?

17 Where was the peace conference to be held?

18 Which old Earth poet is often quoted in ST VI?

19 Which vital piece of evidence is the Enterprise turned upside down for?

20 Which area of the ship do we see for the first time in ST VI?

GENERATIONS

answers page 176

1 Which CT crew members are absent in *Generations*?

2 Which Enterprise is Kirk on board when he disappears?

3 Which regular TNG character is beamed on to Kirk's ship?

4 What is Worf's rank in *Generations*?

5 Which relatives of Picard die in the film?

6 How?

7 What does Data finally get in *Generations*?

8 Who is kidnapped by Soran?

9 How does Soran intend to get the Nexus to come to him?

10 Which regular Klingon duo are killed in *Generations*?

11 What does Picard see in his Nexus fantasy which brings him back to reality?

12 Whereabouts is Kirk living in the Nexus?

13 What happens to the Enterprise-D?

POT POURRI

answers page 176

1 How many actresses played Saavik?

2 Which *Cheers* actress played her first film role in ST II?

3 Who played the shapeshifter in ST VI?

4 Which actor from TNG appeared in ST VI?

5 What character did he play?

6 Which Shakespearian actor played General Chang in ST VI?

7 In which film did Rene Auberjonois (Odo in DS9) appear?

8 When Ilia is abducted by the probe in ST I, one Chief Defalco takes her place, played by actress Marcy Lafferty. What relation was she to William Shatner?

9 Which very famous sci-fi author was employed as a consultant on ST I?

10 Which film sees the destruction of the U.S.S. Grissom?

11 Which film sees the destruction of the Enterprise NCC-1701-A?

12 How long has McCoy been ship's doctor by the time of ST IV?

13 Which film saw Kirk at the helm of a completely new Enterprise?

14 What does the Federation Council President look like?

15 Which famous actress has a major part in *Generations* but does not appear on the credit list?

THE ALIENS

THE ALIENS

MULTIPLE CHOICE

answers page 176

ENSIGN

1 If a Klingon says 'K'Plah' to you, what is he saying?
a] 'Success.'
b] 'Goodbye.'
c] 'Get out of my way!'

2 In which quadrant of the galaxy is the Klingon Homeworld?
a] The Alpha quadrant.
b] The Beta quadrant.
c] The Delta quadrant.

3 What sort of society does Angel One have?
a] Patriarchal.
b] Matriarchal.
c] Fratriarchal.

4 You are being hailed by a Sheliak Consortium space vessel. The captain informs you [incorrectly] that your position in space is a breach of treaty agreements. What is the correct way to reply?
a] 'Red alert! Shields up! Lock phasers and photons on the Sheliak vessel! Fire when ready!'
b] 'According to page 325, paragraph 3, subsection 1a of the Treaty of Armens we are entitled to a two-day recess to consider our options.
c] 'Sheliak vessel. We are on a peaceful science research mission. Please make way.'

CAPTAIN

5 What is unusual about a Betazoid gift box?
a] It is transparent.
b] It is actually a live creature.
c] It has an animated face embedded into it which delivers a message.

6 What is the official title for the leader of the Romulan Empire?

a) Praetor.
b) Emperor.
c) Chancellor.

7 At what age do the inhabitants of Timcin's planet in *Half A Life* commit ritual suicide?
a) 60
b) 65
c) 75

8 It's your first day on a Klingon Vessel as part of the officer exchange program. You make your way to the bridge and the Klingon captain barks 'Hechu'ghos!' at you. What should you do?
a) Raise shields and arm the photons and phasers.
b) Set course.
c) Open hailing frequencies.

ADMIRAL
9 What is Vulcan 'koon-ut-kal-if-fee'?
a) Marriage.
b) Death.
c) The purging of all emotions.

10 Who is M'Rel's son?
a) Worf.
b) Duras.
c) Gowron.

11 A Tamarian delegate is beamed aboard your vessel for important treaty negiotiations. When you greet him in the transporter room, he says: 'Tembu – his arms wide open'. What would be a reasonably sound reply?
a) 'Gorbachev and Reagan at Reykjavik'.
b) 'The Borg and Starfleet at Wolf 359'.
c) 'Red alert! Shields up! Security to transporter room 3!'

12 A web-fingered Zordan approaches you in bar on Starbase 17 and accuses you (in no uncertain terms) of spilling his drink. He insults you, your race, and calls the Federation the Zordan equivalent of a 'dirty public toilet'. What is the best reaction?
a) Apologise profusely and offer to buy him another, if not two more, drinks.
b) Ignore him and hope he will go away.

continued

c) Get angry, turn on him, and accuse his mother of being a member of 'the oldest profession in the world'.

VULCAN HISTORY AND CULTURE

answers page 176

ENSIGN

1 What principle dominates Vulcan existence?

2 What colour is Vulcan blood?

3 What is 'pon farr'?

4 What is the Vulcan 'khatra'?

5 Why is a Vulcan dangerous during 'plak tow'?

6 A 'sehlat' – Spock had one. Lots of Vulcans do. What is it?

7 Sarek's first wife – mother of Sybok – held what rank in the Vulcan monarchy?

8 What letter do male Vulcan names always begin with?

9 What letter do female Vulcan names always begin with?

CAPTAIN

10 Who are the Vishar?

11 A vulcan who has achieved the state of 'kolinahr' has managed what?

12 What is the term when a Vulcan telepathically links with another being?

13 What is Sha Ka Ree in Vulcan mythology?

14 If two Vulcans fight 'ahn-woon' what do they use as weapons?

15 What does a Vulcan 'lirpa' look like?

16 What is fal-tor-pan?

ADMIRAL

17 Who is the symbolic head of Vulcan?

18 In Vulcan history, what part did he play?

19 What is the syndrome suffered by Sarek which causes him to lose control of his emotions?

20 What is the Stone of Gaul?

21 If our blood is iron-based, what is Vulcan blood?

22 What is the Vulcan principle of IDIC?

KLINGON HISTORY AND CULTURE

answers page 176

ENSIGN

1 Why do Klingons have more than their fair share of internal organs?

2 What do Klingons never do when playing poker?

3 In Klingon law, if the father of a family commits a crime, who is equally responsible?

4 Who is Kahless the Unforgettable?

5 What did he do?

6 What is a 'bat'telth'?

7 When a Klingon captain orders another bridge member to 'Bah!' what he is saying?

8 If you call a Klingon a 'baktag' what is likely to happen to you?

9 If you were served Klingon 'gagh' what would it look like?

10 Which nefarious duo tried to start a Klingon civil war?

11 What are their first names?

12 Which race were they affiliated to?

13 Who was made leader of the Klingon High Council after this brief but bloody civil war?

14 Who killed Duras?

15 When a Klingon commander becomes 'weak and unable to perform' what should his first officer do?

16 Where did the Klingons obtain their cloaking device?

17 What word was non-existent in the Klingon language until the Klingons encountered Riva?

CAPTAIN

18 What do the Klingons say for 'goodbye'?

19 Why don't Klingons cry?

20 What colour is Klingon blood?

21 What is a 'd'k tahg'?

22 What is a Klingon Targ?

23 What is the R'uustai?

24 The Ja'chuq is part of which Klingon rite?

25 What must a Klingon do during the Ja'chuq?

26 What would you be doing if you were having 'selon' with a Klingon?

27 Name the three Klingons rescued in *Heart of Glory*.

28 What is Heart of Targ to a Klingon?

29 When a Klingon plans to perform Hegh'bat what is he about to do?

30 Captian Jean-Luc Picard is the only human ever to have been given the Klingon position of...?

31 What was the name of Duras's illegitimate son who challenged Gowron's ascension?

32 What exactly is 'discommendation'?

33 What happens to a Klingon's family if a member is taken prisoner alive?

34 What form of ceremony happens to young warriors at the Age of Ascension?

35 Whose blood stains the Knife of Kirom?

ADMIRAL

36 What is the name of the Klingon homeworld?

37 What is the name of the capital city of the Klingon homeworld?

38 Who is Mooroth in Klingon folklore?

39 By whom, from what, and how was the first bat'telth forged?

40 Who is Gre'thor to the Klingons?

41 What kind of art form is 'Aktuh and Melota'?

42 What is a 'gin'tak'?

43 What is Quie'Tu to religious Klingons?

44 Mythologically speaking, what is Fek'lhr to a Klingon?

45 What is a Klingon's' cha'dich'?

46 What would you do with a 'chech'tluth'?

47 What does 'bat'telth' actually mean?

48 How long has Worf's bat'telth been in the his family?

49 What is the typical age of warriors at the Age of Ascension?

50 Who was the leader of the High Council before the dispute between Gowron and Duras?

51 How did he die?

52 Who, in fact, betrayed Khitomer to the Romulans?

BETAZOID HISTORY AND CULTURE

answers page 177

ENSIGN

1 What do Betazoid women wear for their wedding ceremonies?

2 The majority of Betazoids have telepathic as well as empathic powers. True or false?

3 Which race's minds can Betazoids not read?

4 Which one of Picard's ex-'lady friends' is banned from ever returning to Betazed?

CAPTAIN

5 What is the Betazoid relaxation technique?

6 What is the difference between human and Betazoid menopause?

7 How do Betazoids say 'grace' during a meal?

ADMIRAL

8 How are Betazoid couples generally bonded?

9 During which stage of their lives?

10 Lwaxana Troi is a member of which house of Betazed?

ROMULAN HISTORY AND CULTURE

answers page 177

ENSIGN

1 The Romulan Sela is whose daughter?

2 What colour is Romulan ale?

3 Whom did the Romulans have an alliance with for one hundred years?

CAPTAIN

4 How many homeworlds do the Romulan Empire have?

5 In which quadrant is the main Romulan homeworld?

6 What do the Romulans say for 'goodbye'?

ADMIRAL

7 What do Romulans use to power their ships?

8 In English?

9 Who are the Tal Shiar?

10 What is Vorta Vor in Romulan mythology?

POT POURRI

answers page 177

1 What was the main industry of the planet Minos in *The Arsenal Of Freedom*?

2 What is the main industry of the planet Risa?

3 Who guards *The Last Outpost*?

4 Which planet is the setting for *Encounter At Farpoint*?

5 Which race primarily use 'disrupters' instead of phasers?

6 The Bynars' number system only contains two digits. Which two?

7 What crop do Tribbles eat?

8 What are 'ugly bags of mostly water'?

9 How many Federation legal experts did it take to complete the Sheliak peace treaty?

10 Which race like 'yamack sauce' on their food?

ALIENS: TRUE OR FALSE?

answers page 177

1 The Vorgons hail from the 27th century (*Captain's Holiday*).

2 The Trill are a symbiotic race (*The Host*).

3 Tasha Yar was born on Turkana 5 (*Legacy*).

4 The Aldeans completely cloaked their entire planet (*When The Bough Breaks*).

5 Kevin Uxbridge was really a member of the Q Continuum (*The Survivors*).

6 The Overseer is the God of the Mintakans (*Who Watches The Watchers?*).

7 The Tamarians communicate via similes (*Darmok*).

8 The Bynars' numerical system is based on Base 1 (*11001001*).

9 The Sheliak Corporate are sticklers for rules and precedent (*The Ensigns Of Command*).

10 The name of the evil alien in *Skin Of Evil* was Harman.

11 The Ullians are telepathic historians (*Violations*).

12 Darmok is a mythical figure in Tamarian lore (*Darmok*).

13 The Bandi trapped an alien lifeform and used it as a spacestation (*Encounter At Farpoint*).

14 The Talosians are a race of powerful empathic beings (*The Menagerie* – CT).

15 The Tribbles feed voraciously on corn (*The Trouble With Tribbles* – CT).

16 The Tribbles hate Vulcans (*The Trouble With Tribbles* – CT).

17 The Pakleds are dim-witted but devious scavengers (*Samaritan Snare*).

18 The police in Edonian culture are called 'mediators' (*Justice*).

19 Tarellians are the outcasts of the galaxy because their looks can kill (*Haven*).

20 The Cardassians have always been a militaristic race.

21 The J'naii are an androgynous rac.(*The Outcast*).

22 The Acamarians's peaceful society is marred slightly by the existence of a nomadic branch of their people called the Gatherers (*The Vengeance Factor*).

23 The entire Aldean race were rendered sterile after their planetary cloaking device destroyed their ozone layer and exposed the population to radiation (*When The Bough Breaks*).

24 Andorians have blue skin (*Journey To Babel* – CT).

25 The Angosians created a breed of genetically engineered soldiers who were exiled to a distant moon after the war (*The Hunted*).

26 The Anticans are large and furry but very carnivorous (*Lonely Among Us*).

27 The Douwd are omnipotent beings who look like humans (*The Survivors*).

28 Touching an Elasian's tears will cause you to fall in love with them (*Elaan Of Troyius* – CT).

29 The Yonadans lived on an asteriod when their sun was destroyed (*For The World Is Hollow And I Have Touched The Sky* – CT).

30 The Tamarian language is said to be "ridiculous" (*Darmok*).

31 Orion Animal Women have green skin (*Whom Gods Destroy* – CT).

32 Ornarans are addicted to the drug Felicium, supplied only by the Brekkians (*Symbiosis*).

33 Deltans are bald (ST I).

34 The Denevan were all killed by a nuclear war (*Operation: Annihilate!* – CT).

35 The Gorn are bipedal lizards (*Arena* – CT).

36 The Bringoidi are descended from Scottish farmers (*Up The Long Ladder*).

37 Benzites wear respiratory masks to survive in a Class-M atmosphere (*Coming Of Age*).

38 Cytherians encounter other races by endowing them with the technology to come to them (*Nth Degree*).

39 Bajoran civilization is thousands of years younger than Earth's.

40 Aldebaran Whisky is yellow. (*Relics*).

41 Klingons eat blood pie.

42 The Sheliak spend half the year asleep (*The Ensigns Of Command*).

43 The Halkans are the most peaceful race in the galaxy (*Mirror, Mirror* – CT).

44 The Iconians had a technologically advanced civilisation which died out 200,000 years ago (*Contagion*).

45 The Jarada are a humanoid race who pay fanatical attention to protocol (*Samaritan Snare*).

46 The Kataans stored the entirety of their culture in a single probe (*The Inner Light*).

47 Kerelians have a larger auditory range than humans (*Lessons*).

48 Kitarians have ruffled foreheads, feline eyes, and paws instead of hands (*The Game*).

49 The Crystalline Entity resembles a huge amoeba (*Silicon Avatar*).

50 The Paxans are intensely xenophobic (*Clues*).

BEHIND THE SCENES

BEHIND THE SCENES

ACTORS' NAMES

answers page 178

ENSIGN

1 Who plays Captain Picard?

2 Who plays Riker?

3 Who plays Data?

4 Who plays Sisko?

5 Who plays Beverly Crusher?

6 Who plays Deanna Troi?

7 Who plays Geordi?

8 Who plays Worf?

9 Who plays Wesley Crusher?

10 Who plays Lwaxana Troi?

11 Who plays Chief O'Brien?

12 Who plays Guinan?

13 Who plays Scotty?

14 Who plays Kirk?

15 Who plays Spock?

16 Who plays McCoy?

17 Who plays Sulu?

CAPTAIN

18 Who plays Major Kira?

19 Who plays Tasha Yar?

20 Who plays Dax?

21 Who plays Dr.Bashir?

22 Who plays Odo?

23 Who plays Quark?

24 Who plays Q?

25 Who plays Chekov?

26 Who plays Dr. Pulaski?

27 Who plays Uhura?

28 Who plays Barclay?

ADMIRAL

29 Who plays Vedek Winn?

30 Who plays Vedek Bareil?

31 Who plays Nog?

32 Who plays Rom?

33 Who plays Keiko?

34 Who plays Ensign Ro?

35 Who plays Jake Sisko?

36 Who plays Mr. Homn?

37 Who plays Nurse Ogawa?

38 Who plays Yeoman Janice Rand?

39 Which two actors have played Alexander?

40 Who plays Kai Opaka?

GUEST STARS

answers page 178

ENSIGN

1 Who is the only person to have played himself in an episode of TNG?

2 Which episode did he appear in?

3 Which internationally famous actress and diva played Edith Keeler in *City On The Edge Of Forever*?

4 Majel Roddenberry-Barrett, who plays Lwaxana Troi in TNG, also played which character in CT?

5 And which other 'character' does she play in TNG?

6 Jill Ireland, who, as Leila, Spock fell in love with in *This Side Of Paradise* married which film star?

7 Corbin Bernson, from *LA Law*, plays who in *Deja Q*?

8 Which actor played Makora in the CT episode *The Apple* and later went on to wear a cardigan and chase lots of criminals in cars?

9 Dwight Schultz (Mr. Barclay) made his name in which long-running American action series?

10 What was his character's name?

11 Jean Simmons, who played Admiral Satie in *The Drumhead*, played opposite Marlon Brando and Frank Sinatra in which famous muscial?

CAPTAIN

12 Who did Christopher Lloyd, the wild-eyed totem pole of an actor from *Back To The Future*, play in *ST III: The Search For Spock*?

13 Ricardo Montalban [Khan to us] played a suave foreign fellow in a famous glossy long-running US soap opera. Which one?

14 Daniel Stewart, son of Patrick, played which character in TNG?

15 Which episode saw *Max Headroom* actor Matt Frewer guest star as a visitor from another time?

16 Carel Struycken, who plays Mr Homn, more or less reprises his role in which Hollywood film?

17 Mädchen Amick played one of the forms the shape-shifting bodyguard of Salia took, in which episode?

18 Which series made Mädchen Amick's name?

19 Which actress, famed for roles in *Dynasty* and innumerable TV mini series, played Moriarty's love interest in *Ship In A Bottle*?

20 Ronny Cox [the irascible Captain Jellico in *Chain Of Command*] has made his name playing irascible gits. Name two sci-fi films where he reprises said character?

ADMIRAL

21 Which episode sees a cameo appearance by Mick Fleetwood?

22 Paul Winfield, who played Cpt. Terrell of the U.S.S. Reliant in ST II, also played an incomprehensible alien leader in TNG. Which episode?

23 Which role did Frasier from *Cheers* [Kelsey Grammer] find in the 24th century?

24 Louise Fletcher, who played Nurse Ratchet in *One Flew Over The Cuckoo's Nest*, plays who in DS9?

25 The annoying gregarious Commander Hutchinson in *Starship Mine* is played by the brother of which famous film director?

26 Mark Lenard, who plays Sarek, also played a Romulan in which early CTepisode?

27 And he also played a Klingon in which Trek film?

28 Michelle Phillips, who played Picard's old flame in *We'll Always Have Paris*, was the singer in which popular band?

29 Michelle Forbes (aka Ensign Ro) appeared briefly in another early episode of TNG. Who did she play and in which episode?

30 Wallace Shawn, who plays the Grand Nagus Zek, also played who in The Princess Bride?

ACTORS' LIVES

answers page 179

ENSIGN

1 Denise Crosby, who plays Tasha Yar, is the grand-daughter of which famous crooner?

2 Patrick Stewart has performed a one-man version of which Dickens tale in London's West End and on Broadway?

3 Colm Meaney appeared in a famous Alan Parker film about a Dublin soul band called...?

4 He then went on to play the same character in a BBC film called...?

5 What improbable TV cop did William Shatner play?

6 Which 1960s spy series did Leonard Nimoy guest star in?

CAPTAIN

7 Grace Lee Whitney played which recurring character in CT?

8 The actress who played Dr. Pulaski in TNG's second season appeared in how many CT episodes?

9 Will Wheaton made his big screen debut in an adaptation of a Stephen King short story called…?

10 Patrick Stewart had quite a major role in a British Arthurian film. What was it called?

11 Terry Farrell appeared and indeed was spotted by the DS9 producers in which horror film?

12 Colm Meaney starred alongside Steven Segal in which *Die Hard*-esque thriller?

13 Which episode did Gates McFadden direct?

14 Which famous comedy film starring Ted Danson (among others) did Leonard Nimoy direct?

15 In which film does William Shatner play an hilarious cameo of himself?

16 Which CT actor has guest starred on *Babylon 5*?

17 What Hollywood film starring Jeremy Irons did Genevieve Bujold make her name in?

18 Bebe Neuwirth plays Lilith in *Cheers* but also played a nurse in which TNG episode?

ADMIRAL
19 In which film is a naked Marina Sirtis flogged to death by Faye Dunaway?

20 Armin Shimerman played a Ferengi in which TNG episode?

21 Michelle Forbes – Ensign Ro to you and I – left the series to star in which Hollywood film?

22 Rene Auberjonois (i.e. Odo) played a pious politician in which famous 1980s American sitcom about a black butler?

23 Who is the second highest paid TNG regular (after Patrick Stewart)?

24 Name five episodes that Jonathan Frakes has directed.

25 LeVar Burton directed which two episodes?

26 Patrick Stewart appears in which dire Mel Brooks film?

27 Which finger is James Doohan missing?

28 On which American cop show did Avery Brooks make his name?

29 Which character did he play?

30 Name three episodes Patrick Stewart has directed?

POT POURRI

answers page 179

1 Which Trek film is the TNG theme tune taken from?

2 Who was in the most CT episodes? Kirk or Spock?

3 Where does the Vulcan hand signal originate?

4 Who is the character Geordi La Forge named after?

5 What was the name of the pilot episode of CT?

6 Which two cast members of the pilot went on to appear in CT?

7 How many TNG episodes were there in total (two-parters count as two)?

8 How many CT episodes were there in total?

9 How many episodes are there per season in DS9?

10 Which anti-Starfleet organisation has crew members aboard the U.S.S. Voyager?

11 What is unique about Voyager's medical officer?

12 In which order do the actors appear in the opening credits of TNG?

13 Gene Roddenberry donated his middle name as the christian name of which crew member?

14 It's called the 'conn' in TNG but what was it called in CT?

15 Which author wrote *Wolf In The Fold* and numerous other CT episodes but is better known for creating Antony Perkins and Alfred Hitchcock's best known film?

16 During which season of TNG did Gene Roddenberry die?

17 During the filming of which episode?

18 How many episodes on average are there per season of TNG?

19 Which CT regular provided the voice for the M-5 computer in *The Ultimate Computer*?

20 What is the Trekker term for TNG and DS9 dialogue which descends into unnecessary scientific gobbledegook?

21 Recite Kirk's monologue from the start of every CT episode (including pauses).

22 Recite Picard's monologue from the start of every TNG episode (including pauses).

23 Who was the "Great Bird of the Galaxy"?

24 Who is the producer of TNG and DS9?

25 Who is the executive producer?

BEHIND THE SCENES: TRUE OR FALSE?

answers page 179

1 The writers of TNG planned to make Geordi an alien in the seventh season to spice up his character.

2 Data no longers plays the character of Sherlock Holmes in later episodes of TNG because the Arthur Conan Doyle estate wanted mega-bucks for the licence.

3 The DS9 producers killed off Kai Opaka early into the first season of DS9 because they were disappointed with Camille Saviola's performance.

4 Patrick Stewart didn't want to stay on for a seventh season of TNG but was lured back with promises of a lucrative film contract.

5 Patrick Stewart stormed out of a live *Good Morning America* broadcast because he took exception to the programme's weatherman appearing as a Starfleet officer in a brief sketch on the Ten Forward set.

6 Genevieve Bujold, cast to play Captain Janeaway in *Voyager*, walked out after a week of filming the pilot episode.

7 Patsy Kensit and Linda Wagner were seriously considered for the role of the captain in the new Trek series.

8 Originally, Saavik stayed behind on Vulcan at the beginning of ST IV because she was carrying Spock's baby.

9 In the DS9 episode *If Wishes Were Horses*, O'Brien's daughter was initially going to conjure up a leprechaun after O'Brien had told her a traditional Irish folktale. Colm Meaney, however, objected to this racist Irish stereotype, so it was taken out.

10 The reason the Enterprise never performs a saucer separation outside a few episodes is because the effect is too expensive and slows the pace of the story somewhat (not to mention it's a crap idea).

11 Bill Shatner wears a hair-piece.

12 Leonard Nimoy was Paramount Studio's first choice to produce TNG when it was first being mooted in the mid-eighties. Gene Roddenberry was actually third down the list.

13 'I have to tell you why I despise you' said Nichelle Nichols to William Shatner in real life.

14 Allegedly, James Doohan doesn't like William Shatner and doesn't want to speak to him ever again.

15 When Paramount secretly coded Trek scripts to see who was leaking them to fans, they found that Gene Roddenberry was the main culprit.

SEEN EVERY EPISODE?

For each series of TNG, match the title with the brief plot summary.

SEASON ONE

answers page 180

1 *Encounter At Farpoint*

2 *The Naked Now*

3 *Code Of Honour*

4 *The Last Outpost*

5 *Where No One Has Gone Before*

6 *Lonely Among Us*

7 *Justice*

8 *Battlines*

9 *Hide and Q*

10 *Haven*

11 *The Big Goodbye*

12 *Datalore*

13 *Angel One*

14 *11001001*

15 *Too Short A Season*

16 *When The Bough Breaks*

17 *Home Soil*

18 *Coming Of Age*

19 *Heart Of Glory*

20 *The Arsenal Of Freedom*

21 *Symbiosis*

22 *Skin Of Evil*

23 *We'll Always Have Paris*

24 *Conspiracy*

25 *The Neutral Zone*

a) Wesley steps on some flowers and is sentenced to die.

b) Binary numbers.

c) Three Klingon fugitives.

d) Drunken crew. Tasha sleeps with Data.

e) Picard possessed by alien cloud.

f) Matriachal society and virus.

g) Terraformed crystal alien is unhappy.

h) Planet which sells weapons.

i) First episode.

j) Paris.

k) Tasha Yar kidnapped. Forced to fight chief's wife.

l) Academy Entrance Exam.

m) Riker as Q.

n) Enterprise kids kidnapped.

o) Troi to get married.

p) Something's afoot in Starfleet.

q) The Traveller.

r) One race sells drugs to the other race.

s) Picard as Dixon Hill.

t) The Romulans.

u) Portal and the Ferengi.

v) The old Admiral gets really young.

w) Tasha dies.

x) Data's brother.

y) Damon Bok and the mind control device.

SEASON TWO

answers page 180

1   *The Child*

2   *Where Silence Has Lease*

3   *Elementary, My Dear Data*

4   *The Outrageous Okona*

5   *Loud As A Whisper*

6   *The Schizoid Man*

7   *Unnatural Selection*

8   *A Matter Of Honor*

9   *The Measure Of A Man*

10   *The Dauphin*

11   *Contagion*

12   *The Royale*

13   *Time Squared*

14   *The Icarus Factor*

15   *Pen Pals*

16 *Q Who*

17 *Samaritan Snare*

18 *Up The Long Ladder*

19 *Manhunt*

20 *The Emmissary*

21 *Peak Performance*

22 *Shades Of Grey*

a) Enterprise experimented on by alien cloud.

b) Data on trial for his life.

c) Geordi kidnapped by thickies.

d) Wesley fancies an alien shape-changer.

e) Data possessed by mad scientist.

f) Data saves his alien friend.

g) The Borg!

h) Deanna gets pregnant.

i) K'Ehlyr.

j) Data wants to laugh.

k) Lwaxana Troi.

l) Data as Holmes.

m) Irish farmers in the shuttle bay.

n) The Yamato gets destroyed.

o) Riker's dad.

p) The Enterprise in battle exercises.

q) Pulaski gets old.

r) Deaf and dumb mediator.

s) The crew are trapped in a Vegas hotel.

t) Two Picards.

u) Riker flashes back on the entire series.

v) Riker on a Klingon exchange.

SEASON THREE

answers page 180

1   Evolution

2   The Ensigns Of Command

3   The Survivors

4   Who Watches The Watchers?

5   The Bonding

6   Booby Trap

7   The Enemy

8   The Price

9   The Vengeance Factor

10 The Defector

11 The Hunted

12 The High Ground

13 Deja Q

14 A Matter Of Perspective

15 Yesterday's Enterprise

16 The Offspring

17 Sins Of The Father

18 *Allegiance*

19 *Captain's Holiday*

20 *Tin Man*

21 *Hollow Pursuits*

22 *The Most Toys*

23 *Sarek*

24 *Ménage A Troi*

25 *Transfigurations*

26 *The Best Of Both Worlds I*

a) Jeremy's mother comes back from the dead.

b) An invincible soldier avoids the Enterprise.

c) Picard kidnapped and examined in a cell.

d) Picard is a God to the proto-Vulcans.

e) The Spy Who Came In From The Neutral Zone.

f) Vash on Risa.

g) Kevin and Rishon Uxbridge.

h) Worf's discommendation.

i) The Enterprise is caught in a 10,000-year-old snare.

j) Q as a mortal.

k) Tam Elbrun and a dying space creature.

l) Data stolen by collector.

m) Data to convince colonists to get out.

n) John Doe turns into an energy creature.

o) Geordi and Romulan make friends on nasty planet.

p) Spock's dad.

q) Barclay and his holodeck programs.

r) A wormhole is up for grabs.

s) Troi and her mother kidnapped by Ferengi.

t) Picard and Bev captured by terrorists.

u) Riker kills a biological assassin.

v) The Borg are back.

w) Riker accused of murder. Trial by holodeck.

x) Time Travel. War with Klingons. Tasha Yar. Guinan.

y) Wesley's nanites nearly nobble the ship.

z) Data's daughter.

SEASON FOUR
answers page 180

1 *The Best Of Both Worlds II*

2 *Family*

3 *Brothers*

4 *Suddenly Human*

5 *Remember Me*

6 *Legacy*

7 *Reunion*

8 *Future Imperfect*

9 *Final Mission*

10 *The Loss*

11 *Data's Day*

12 *The Wounded*

13 *Devil's Due*

14 *Clues*

15 *First Contact*

16 *Galaxy's Child*

17 *Night Terrors*

18 *Identity Crisis*

19 *Nth Degree*

20 *Q-pid*

21 *The Drumhead*

22 *Half A Life*

23 *The Host*

24 *The Mind's Eye*

25 *In Theory*

26 *Redemption I*

a) Data gets a girlfriend.

b) Locutus of Borg.

c) K'Ehlyr's back with Worf's son.

d) Goddess comes back to get her planet.

e) Enterprise mistaken for alien baby's mother.

f) Timcin must die at 60.

g) Data takes control of the Enterprise.

h) Picard and the crew gently introduce alien planet to Federation.

i) Tasha's sister.

j) Troi minus empathic powers.

k) The crew in Sherwood Forest.

l) Maverick federation ship attacks Cardies.

m) Picard amongst the vineyards.

n) Crusher in love with a Trill.

o) Crew not getting any dream sleep. Except Troi.

p) Diary of Data. O'Brien gets married.

q) A witch hunt aboard the Enterprise.

r) Geordi turns into an alien.

s) Human boy found on alien ship.

t) Geordi brainwashed by Romulans.

u) Worf goes to get back his family's honour.

v) Barclay as super-genius.

w) Wes and Picard crash on desert planet.

x) Bev and her static warp bubble.

y) The crew all lose a day – except Data

z) Riker loses sixteen years.

SEASON FIVE

answers page 180

1   *Redemption II*

2   *Darmok*

3   *Ensign Ro*

4   *Silicon Avatar*

5   *Disaster*

6 *The Game*

7 *Unification I*

8 *Unification II*

9 *A Matter Of Time*

10 *New Ground*

11 *Hero Worship*

12 *Violations*

13 *The Masterpiece Society*

14 *Conundrum*

15 *Power Play*

16 *Ethics*

17 *The Outcast*

18 *Cause And Effect*

19 *The First Duty*

20 *Cost Of Living*

21 *The Perfect Mate*

22 *Imaginary Friend*

23 *I, Borg*

24 *The Next Phase*

25 *The Inner Light*

26 *Time's Arrow I*

a) O'Brien, Data, Troi are possessed.

b) Spock has defected.

c) Feisty young Bajoran joins the crew.

d) Boring one with Alexander and Lwaxana Troi.

e) Spock hasn't defected.

f) Wesley in deep trouble at SFA.

g) Incomprehensible aliens who speak in metaphor.

h) Picard chaperones the ideal woman.

i) Worf saves his family's bacon.

j) The crew loses its memory but gains a new officer.

k) The Crystalline Entity gets killed.

l) Riker falls in love with androgynous alien.

m) Enterprise causes problem in genetically engineered society.

n) Traveller in time visits the Enterprise.

o) A girl's 'little friend' comes to terrifying life.

p) Worf and Alexander having problems.

q) A single Borg is converted to individualism.

r) Enterprise caught in a time loop.

s) Troi is mentally raped.

t) Geordi and Ro become invisible.

u) Data is role model for distraught boy.

v) Picard lives an entire life in 22 minutes.

w) Worf breaks his back.

x) Riker brings back his addiction from Risa.

y) Data's head found in San Francisco.

z) The Enterprise is badly damaged.

answers page 180

23 *Rightful Heir*

24 *Second Chances*

25 *Timescape*

26 *Descent I*

a) Amanda is a Q.

b) Kahless returns.

c) People are disappearing in the night.

d) Two Rikers.

e) Bev's whodunnit with metaphasic shielding.

f) Troi is a Romulan.

g) Picard and chums turned into children.

h) Picard dies and lives again.

i) Scotty.

j) A remake of Laura.

k) Riker's reality is shattered.

l) Worf and Alex in Wild West with Data.

m) Picard in love. Problems.

n) Secret in DNA.

o) Barclay gets scared of transporters.

p) Mark Twain on the Enterprise.

q) Exocomps.

r) Picard captured by Cardassians.

s) Enterprise frozen in time.

t) Die Hard in space.

u) Data dreams.

v) Troi is possessed by negative emotions.

w) Data feels his first emotion – anger.

x) Picard interrogated by Cardassians.

y) Worf doesn't find his father.

z) Moriarty again.

———————————————————————— *SEASON SEVEN*

answers page 180

17 *Masks*

18 *Eye Of The Beholder*

19 *Genesis*

20 *Journey's End*

21 *Firstborn*

22 *Bloodlines*

23 *Emergence*

24 *Pre-emptive Strike*

25 *All Good Things I & II*

a) Data's mother.

b) Lwaxana's deepest secret revealed.

c) Worf's foster brother.

d) Troi has a weird empathic experience.

e) The Enterprise turns into an ancient city.

f) Ro returns.

g) Picard goes undercover as a pirate.

h) Picard's son?

i) The Enterprise's computer gives birth.

j) Data dreams about Troi cake.

k) Federation cloaking device.

l) Worf experiences multiple universes.

m) Bev's family secret.

n) Three bizarre ambassadors.

o) Warp drives are bad - official.

p) Data escapes Lore's control.

q) The crew turn into monkeys.

r) Data forgets about radiation.

s) Riker goes undercover as a pirate as well.

t) Native American Indians.

u) Picard and Bev get it on.

v) Geordi and virtual reality.

w) The Last Episode Ever.

x) Alexander from the future.

y) The ship's crew from a different perspective.

QUOTES

answers page 181

For each quote, give who was speaking, to whom, in which episode and in what context.

ENSIGN

1 'A surprise party! I hate surprise parties! I would never do that to you.'

2 'You've told me what to eat and what to think and what to say – and then when I show a glimmer of independent thought, you strap me down, you inject me with drugs and you call it a treatment!'

3 'I am not a merry man!'

4 'He's dead, Jim.'

5 'Men do not roar – women roar. Then they hurl heavy objects and claw at you.'

6 'Good tea. Nice house.'

7 'Not even a bite on the cheek for old time's sake?'

8 'Felus Cattus is your taxonomic nomenclature,
An endothermic quadruped, carnivorous by nature.'

9 'Could you please continue the petty bickering. I find it most intriguing.'

10 'Pity, you might have learned an interesting lesson, macrohead with a microbrain.'

11 'We hoped our probe would encounter someone in the future – someone who could be a teacher, someone who could tell the others about us.'

12 'Very well. He's an Admiral. I'm a captain – I cannot *force* you to disobey his orders. Therefore I will have to remain in the dark on this mission, and I will just have to trust that you will not let

Pressman put this ship at unnecessary risk. And if I find that this trust has been misplaced then I will have to re-evaluate the command structure of this ship. Dismissed!'

13 'Starfleet was founded to seek out new life...well there it sits.'

14 'I will still fill you with crumpet, Madam.'

15 'Me?!'

CAPTAIN

16 'Captain, we are receiving 285,000 hails!'

17 'Here's to ye, lads!'

18 'By golly, Jim, I'm beginning to think I can cure a rainy day.'

19 'When one is the penalty box, tears are permitted.'

20 'Oh, very clever, Worf. Eat any good books lately?'

21 'And if my mother had wheels, she'd be a wagon.'

22 'When I am pricked, do I not leak?'

23 'Your ambushes would be more successful if you would bath regularly.'

24 '...And get that fish out of the ready room!'

25 'Mister La Forge, when I left this ship it was in one piece. I would appreciate your returning it to me in the same condition.'

26 'It is the sign of La Forge'.

27 'I hate to be indiscreet, but who's the father?'

28 'We'll have this fixed up in time fer supper.'

29 'Maybe I can get one of the females to breastfeed you.'

30 'Revenge is a dish best served cold.'

31 'There was a young lady from Venus,
Whose body was shaped like a –'

ADMIRAL
32 'I did not play with toys!'

33 'I'm a doctor, not a mechanic.'

34 'I'm a doctor, not a bricklayer.'

35 'I'm a doctor, not an escalator.'

36 'Nice legs...for a human.'

37 'I don't like to lose.'

38 'What happened to your hair?'

39 'A warrior's drink!'

40 'Beam me up, Scotty.'

41 'I have the feeling I used to be the jealous type.'

42 'I should have done this a long time ago.'

43 'You're getting on my nerves – now I have them.'

44 'Trouble.'

45 'Bingo!'

46 'Fate protects fools, little children, and ships called Enterprise.'

47 'I can sense something, but I'm not sure what.'

48 'If winning is not important, Commander, then why keep score?'

49 'I was just hoping you were going to ask me that, Captain. I just love to scan for life forms.'

50 'The needs of the many...far outweigh...the needs of...the few.'

WORDS

answers page 185

Match the word or phrase to the correct definition.

1	Nacelle	20	Neural Implant
2	Neutrino Beacon	21	53 years
3	The Phase	22	The Ghorusda Disaster
4	Ritter Scale	23	Containment Field
5	Tal-Shaya	24	Dilithium Crystals
6	Tal Shiar	25	Eugenics War
7	T-9	26	Inverson's Disease
8	Trilithium Resin	27	Kosinksi
9	Dr. Reyga	28	The Khitomer Massacre
10	Dal'Rok	29	Krieger Waves
11	Yangtze Kiang	30	Locator Bomb
12	Surah	31	M-5
13	Static Warp Bubble	32	Age Of Resolution
14	Strategema	33	Agonizer
15	Temporal Causuality Loop	34	Baryon Particles
16	Tomalak	35	Biofilter
17	The Jem'hadar	36	Charnoch's Comedy Cabaret
18	Acts Of Cumberland	37	Chula
19	Tuvok	38	Cloaking Device

39 Boothby

40 Dimensional Shifting

41 Tritanium

42 221B Baker Street

43 Code 47

44 Galorndon Core.

45 Andorians

46 The Nose

47 Admiral Quinn

48 Psychotronic Stability Exam

49 Felicium

50 Jo'Bril

A Where Sherlock Holmes, Data's alter-ego, lives.

B Betazoid female menopause.

C Warp field generators on either side of a starship.

D Toxic waste by-product of warp engines, and a volatile explosive.

E A DS9 Runabout.

F A universe within a universe experienced by Beverly Crusher.

G Kolrami beat Data at this in *Peak Performance*.

H The Enterprise was caught for 17.4 days in one of these.

I Ferocious Gamma quadrant inhabitants.

J A forcefield placed around an object or person.

K Essential for warp travel.

L Romulan attack on a Klingon outpost which Starfleet vessels tried to prevent. Engendered the peace between the Klingon Empire and the Federation.

M Part of a transporter system which removes known viruses from the body of the person beaming up.

N Vulcan method for painless execution.

O Romulan secret police.

P Energy Converter, stolen by the Ferengi in *The Last Outpost*.

Q The Ferengi scientist who invented metaphasic shielding.

R A fearsome cloud which threatened a Bajoran village.

S Recurring Romulan character in TNG.

T Bio-electrical implants found in Geordi's skull.

U Disastrous first contact by Federation which set policy on future first contact operations.

V A global Earth war in 1996 involving Khan.

W Admiral Mark Jameson suffers from this in *Too Short A Season*.

X Supposed warp drive 'expert'.

Y Mega-computer invented by Richard Daystrom.

Z Sixty: the age at which inhabitants of Kaelon-2 commit ritual suicide.

AA Transported down for Geordi to find on a planet ravaged by electromagnetic storms in *The Enemy*.

BB Used to measure interstellar radiation.

CC Title for the leader of a Bajoran community.

DD The Federation Rulebook on Sentience.

EE Vulcan security officer on U.S.S. Voyager.

FF How long there had been no Federation contact with the Romulans at the start of TNG.

GG A new form of power source invented by Dr. Nel Apgar.

HH Pheromone-seeking Ferengi explosive device.

II   Device used in the 'mirror' universe for punishment.

JJ   Accumulated by a starship after extensive warp travel.

KK   The game the Wadi bring to DS9.

LL   A transporter method ruled out by Starfleet as lethal.

MM Fish-like aliens from Pacifica.

NN   Nasty Takaran scientist who killed Dr.Reyga and nearly killed Bev in *Suspicions*.

OO   Planet where Romulan ship crashed in *The Enemy*.

PP   For Captain's eyes only.

QQ   Bar recreated on the holodeck by Data to explore the notion of 'comedy'.

RR   Makes ships invisible to the sensors and to the eye.

SS   The grounds-keeper at SFA.

TT   The hardest substance known to man.

WW Used in Klingon foreplay.

XX   Possessed by parasitic worm aliens in *Conspiracy*.

YY   Dreaded by Wesley during his SFA entrance exam.

ZZ   Drug the Ornarans are addicted to.

ACADEMY ENTRANCE EXAM

The following test is just an overview of what you should expect from a full entrance exam. The test centres on the U.S.S. Enterprise-D, captained by Jean-Luc Picard, as this is the current flagship of the Federation and encapsulates, in its complex structure and running procedure, a thorough test-bed for would-be cadets. You will be tested on its history, its specifications, its computer systems and deck layout, as well as background questions on Starfleet history, technology, and procedure.

This test is difficult. Do not attempt to take this exam unless you have achieved Admiralcy or, at least, high-level Captaincy in the previous tests. You will receive no clues. Approximately correct answers may be admissible, but only at the discretion of the examiner.

There may be trick questions.

Good luck.

THE USS ENTERPRISE

OVERVIEW

answers page 185

1 What class is the NCC-1701-D?

2 Where was the Enterprise built?

3 Who designed the NCC-1701-D's engines?

4 When was it commissioned into service (Earth Year)?

5 What is the name of the Enterprise's sister ship?

6 Who captained the Enterprise's sister ship?

7 Where was it lost?

8 What are the Enterprise's primary mission directives:
a) Exploration, research, diplomacy, defense, enactment of Star Fleet Policy.
b) Exploration, research, diplomacy, offensive maneouvres, liaison with Star Fleet allies.
c) Exploration, research, diplomacy, information retrieval, flagship of the Federation.

STATISTICS

answers page 185

9 How many full-time crew members are there aboard the Enterprise?

10 What is the maximum emergency crew?

11 How much habitable space does the Enterprise-D contain?

12 What is its sustainable cruise velocity?

13 What is its maximum (on paper) warp velocity?

14 How many phaser arrays does the Enterprise have?

15 How many photon torpedo launchers does the Enterprise have?

16 What is the maximum range of a photon torpedo?

17 How many classes of probe are there?

18 How many shuttle bays does the Enterprise have?

GEOGRAPHY

answers page 185

19 On which deck is the main computer core located?

20 On which deck is the arboretum located?

21 On which deck is the main bridge located?

22 On which deck are the officers' quarters located?

23 On which deck is sickbay located?

24 On which deck is the main shuttle bay located?

25 On which deck is main engineering located?

26 On which deck is the Battle Bridge located?

27 Where is the captain's yacht?

28 What is it generally used for?

29 Where are lifeforms considered a threat to the ship held?

30 What is the standard mode of inter-deck transport on a starship such as the Enterprise?

CREW SYSTEMS

answers page 186

31 On the bridge there are five main workstations. In default configuration they are:
a) Science 1, Tactical, Mission Operations, Environment, Engineering
b) Science 1, Science 2, Mission Operations, Environment, Engineering
c) Science 1, Science 2, Tactical, Mission Operations, Engineering.

32 Which aspect of the Enterprise's operation is controlled by the 'CONN' ?

33 Which aspect of the Enterprise's operation is controlled by 'OPPS'?

34 Which aspect of the Enterprise's operation is controlled by TACTICAL?

35 What are the main responsibilities of the officer at the Conn?
a) Navigation, autopilot supervision, manual flight operations.
b) Navigation, tractor beam operation, autopilot supervision, and manual flight.
c) Navigation.

36 What are the Enterprise's windows made out of?

HISTORY

answers page 186

37 What class was the NCC-1701-A?

38 Who originally captained the NCC-1701-A before Captain James T. Kirk?

39 What was the maximum warp of the first NCC-1701-A?

40 What was the average cruise warp speed for the same ship?

41 How many phaser banks did it have?

42 How many photon launchers did it have?

43 How many crew members?

44 How many science labs did the Enterprise have?

45 What did the CT Enterprise-A originally use for data storage?

46 Who captained the NCC-1701-C?

47 What happened to the NCC-1701-C?

48 What class of ship was the Enterprise-C?

STARFLEET REGULATIONS
answers page 186

49 Which two officers can authorise a self-destruct?

50 What is standard procedure in the event of a warp containment breach?

51 Which is higher – security level one or seven?

52 Which is more exhaustive – a level one or a level three diagnostic?

53 Which is a worse emergency – Code 1 or Code 2?

54 What does Code 1 signify?

55 What code designates an incoming secret message?

56 How many pips does an Ensign wear?

57 How many pips does a Lt. Commander have?

58 How many pips does a Captain have?

59 What is the name of the rule that every member of Starfleet must never break?

60 What does that rule strictly prohibit?

61 Which alien alcoholic beverage is banned by the Federation?

STARFLEET INSTITUTIONS

answers page 186

62 Which city is Starfleet HQ based in?

63 What is Starfleet's central organisation of scientific research?

64 According to Lt. Comm. Bruce Maddox, what three characteristics does a sentient being exhibit?

65 The Starfleet Academy flight exercise area is located in the proximity of which planet?

66 What is the annual SFA dance called?

67 The motto for Starfleet Academy is '*ex astris, scienta*'. What does it mean?

STARFLEET HISTORY

answers page 186

68 What treaty prevents the Federation from developing a cloaking device?

69 Who was the treaty signed by?

70 Who is the father of 24th century computer technology?

71 How did Starfleet honour him?

72 What is the significance of Wolf 359 in Starfleet history?

73 How many starships were destroyed?

74 How many Starfleet personnel and their families were lost?

75 Who invented the first warp drive?

THE GALAXY
answers page 186

76 What is the name of our galaxy?

77 In what sector is Earth located?

78 How many quadrants is the Galaxy split into?

79 Name them.

80 What is a small black hole called?

81 Approximately how many planets are affiliated to the United Federation Of Planets?

82 How many neutral zones border Federation space?

83 An Astronomical unit – or AU – refers to what distance in Earth's solar system?

84 What unit of measurement is used to gauge power?

85 Why is intergalatic travel impossible?

STARFLEET TECHNOLOGY
answers page 187

86 What is the standard medium for space communications?

87 What percentage of Warp 1.0 is full impulse velocity?

88 What is the accepted method of clearing a starship of tachyon particles?

89 What is the maximum safe range of a transporter?

90 What is the ratio between matter and antimatter in a warp engine?

91 However, if the matter and antimatter tanks are nine tenths depleted, what is the inter-mix ratio required to reach a Starbase 100 light years away at Warp 8?

92 What device can assist transporters when beaming through interference?

93 What is an active tachyon beam grid useful for detecting?

94 What is the name of the material found in all warp engines which controls the flow of matter/antimatter?

95 Why is this substance so special in the matter/antimatter environment of a warp core?

96 What device isolates dangerous antimatter materials and prevents them from destroying the ship?

97 What is the name for the two parallel warp field generators on either side of a starship?

98 What is the primary software and data storage medium on Starfleet vessels?

99 What is the name of the small computers Starfleet personnel carry about their person to store and relate data?

100 What does the acronym stand for?

101 What device allows all species of all planets to communicate with each other?

102 What is the name of the standard Starfleet hand-held computer and sensor device?

103 What can a cloaked vessel generally not do?

104 Which race developed the cloaking device first?

105 What are the three levels of phaser setting?

106 Which device prevents a starship from toppling from side to side under severe gravometric stress?

THEORETICAL SCIENCE
answers page 187

107 What is metaphasic shielding?

108 What is a Soliton Wave?

109 What essentially is a wormhole?

110 Which form of teleportation was ditched by Starfleet a hundred years ago?

111 Why?

112 What, theoretically speaking, could a phased and cloaked ship do?

113 Why can a starship never travel at warp 10?

114 What is a Dyson Sphere?

STARFLEET SPACE VESSELS
answers page 187

115 What are Transponder Codes?

116 What is the name for the highly secret over-ride code for each Starfleet vessel?

117 Name three classes of Federation ship.

GENERAL TECHNOLOGY

answers page 187

118 What is the nearest the Starfleet personnel come to an alcoholic beverage?

119 Which race invented it?

120 What produces food in the 24th century?

121 Name the two types of replicators.

122 What is the 24th century equivalent of a syringe?

EARTH HISTORY

answers page 187

Match the dates to the significant events.

1 1996

2 2040

3 2042

4 2078

5 2079

6 2150

7 2160

8 2180

9 2230

10 2233

11 2218

12 2264

13 2277

14 2285

15 2271

16 2293

17 2328

18 2344

19 2367

20 2369

a) James T. Kirk born.

b) The V'Ger probe threatens Earth.

c) The Klingon moon of Praxis explodes.

d) Nuclear war on Earth

e) Eugenics War.

f) War against the Romulans. Treaty of Algeron established.

g) Commander B. Sisko assigned to Deep Space Nine.

h) The Khitomer massacre.

i) Australia joins the World Federation.

j) TV dies out.

k) Enterprise A destroyed in orbit around Genesis planet.

l) Spock born.

m) War with the Borg.

n) Individual ship's insignia replaced by the Enterprise logo.

o) Disastrous first contact with the Klingons.

p) Romulan Neutral Zone established.

q) The Post Atomic Horror Court.

r) Professional baseball dies out.

s) Captain James T. Kirk departs on his first five-year mission.

t) Cardassia annexes Bajor.

ANSWERS

ANSWERS

CLASSIC TREK

MULTIPLE CHOICE

1 c. **2** b. **3** c. **4** a. **5** b. **6** c. **7** a. **8** c. **9** c.

ENTERPRISE CREW

1 Security . **2** Janice. **3** The ubiquitous transporter chief. **4** A box of Tribbles. **5** An insult about his beloved Enterprise. **6** Pavel. **7** Ensign. **8** Kirk. **9** Spock. **10** Scotty. **11** Kirk and Spock. **12** Because Nomad wipes her memory. **13** By acting illogically and causing it a 'nervous breakdown'. **14** Spock. **15** Threatens the bridge with a sword. **16** Sulu and Scott. **17** Kirk, McCoy, Scotty and Uhura. **18** Spock. **19** By getting it drunk. **20** Scotty. **21** The alternate Chekov. **22** By exposing them to human sensations. **23** Botany. **24** *Amok Time*. **25** Irena. **26** Andreivich. **27** Sulu. **28** His shock at seeing a dead body on the planet caused a surge of adrenaline which protected him.

CHARACTERS

1 Dr. Richard Daystrom. **2** Redjac or Jack The Ripper. **3** An alien computer. **4** Because he is crippled and they can provide him with a better life. **5** Beautiful women. **6** Nomad. **7** Khan. **8** Salt. **9** Jack The Ripper. **10** He had a heart-attack. **11** Because his looks could literally kill. **12** Harcourt Fenton Mudd. **13** Commodore Matthew Decker. **14** To protect its young. **15** An immortal human who has lived many famous previous lives – Da Vinci, etc. **16** General Trelane. **17** Kollos. **18** Because it had merged with an alien probe designed to collect sterilized soil samples and then put 2 and 2 together and made 7. **19** To recruit fertile males to propagate her race. **20** So he could tell her to shut up. **21** The ability to change shape. **22** He went insane. **23** A Nazi regime. **24** Melakon, his aide. **25** Cyrano Jones. **26** Because he bears a grudge against Kirk and hopes Kirk will be court-martialled for 'killing' him. **27** Cpt. Tracey. **28** Apollo has an enlarged gland in his chest. **29** T'Pau. **30** Achilles. **31** Because of a food shortage. **32** Because he had left the Earth.

PLOTS

1 At puberty. **2** A crew member of a previous ship left a book about gangsters on the planets 100 years before. **3** It destroys the Excalibur while thinking an exercise was real. **4** His daughter, Lenore Karidian. **5** She was killing off the witnesses of her father's sordid past. **6** Telepathically. **7** The Roman Age. **8** That the grain was poisoned. **9** They age rapidly. **10** Blood. **11** By destroying his temple with phaser fire. **12** Lots of children. **13** Plato. **14** Fear. **15** An electrical cloud formed by the life essences of long dead Zetarians. **16** The Klingons. **17** To see if it can be colonised. **18** An alien biological weapon. **19** Because the alien entity Gorgon has supressed their grief. **20** Vina (the blonde woman). **21** Miners. **22** The Klingons. **23** Transporter malfunction. **24** By transporting them to a nearby planet. **25** The Doomsday machine destroys that planet too. **26** By flying a shuttle craft right into its mouth. **27** No. **28** They flew an entire starship into its mouth. **29** Yes. **30** An interplanetary insanity epidemic. **31** Fight. **32** Because it fed off negative emotions. **33** He's forced to live with androids of his wife. **34** To experience the emotions of the enterprise's crew. **35** Absorbed them into its society by removing their individuality. **36** Everything – fruit included – was poisonous to humans. **37** They want to use its weapons. **38** Because of the environmental conditions of the mine. **39** An errant asteroid. **40** Hostility. **41** With the illegal venus drug. **42** The Son (Of God). They were prototype Christians. **43** They were protected by the Guardian. **44** Knowledge. **45** Clark Gable. **46** Ultraviolet light. **47** A bluff conceived by Captain Kirk which implied that the Enterprise had a built-in self-destruct 'Corbomite' system to destroy attacking vessels. **48** In a car crash.

OBSERVATION

1 Shakespeare. **2** Their eyes turn silver and they gain enhanced psychic powers. **3** A dwarven human. **4** A serpent-like head lurching out from the rock. **5** A UFO. **6** Disembodied brains. **7** As a giant green hand holding the ship motionless. **8** The Vulcan Nerve Pinch and 'He's dead Jim'. **9** Phaser rifle. **10** The I.S.S. Enterprise. **11** Stella. **12** A giant amoeba. **13** The crew's phasers. **14** Lead an expedition into space. **15** The Guardian Of Forever in *City On The Edge Of Forever* (a staggering 6 billion years old no less). **16** The Body. **17** Small, tetrahedral blocks. **18** 50,000 years. **19** Surah (Romulan leader), Abe Lincoln, Colonel Green (of Earth), Kahless the Unforgettable (Klingon). **20** 500 years.

CAPTAIN KIRK: PERSONAL LOG

1 Tiberius. **2** Khan Singh. **3** As a father figure. **4** Fight in single combat. **5** McCoy injects him with a powerful sedative. **6** Love. **7** Sleeping gas. **8** By self-destructing the Enterprise. **9** Because Earth's history and future would otherwise have been changed for the worse. **10** Three. **11** Yeoman Rand. **12** For jettisoning a pod with a crew member inside. **13** He was the youngest captain in Starfleet history. **14** A deadly cloudlike creature he could have destroyed 11 years before. **15** To use all the alien (to him) diseases in Kirk's bloodstream to curb his planet's overpopulation problem. **16** Abraham Lincoln. **17** *The Paradise Syndrome.* **18** Because he had amnesia. **19** Janice Lester. **20** An old flame. **21** Riverside, Iowa. **22** George. **23** Sam. **24** By saving the pregnant Eleen from death. **25** Its creator, Jackson Roykirk. **26** By convincing it that it is imperfect and should destroy itself. **27** By telling the probe it was in error in mistaking Kirk for its creator. **28** By taking a poisoned dart intended for Kirk.

SCIENCE OFFICER SPOCK: PERSONAL LOG

1 Strange spores fired from indigenous alien plants. **2** Sarek. **3** Ambassador. **4** Nurse Chapel. **5** The alternate Spock had a beard. **6** By using the Vulcan's hitherto unknown extra eyelid. **7** Kirk. **8** To steal a Romulan cloaking device. **9** Because Romulans look exactly like Vulcans. **10** A tricorder. **11** Because the Enterprise is under threat from an Orion ship. **12** His brain. **13** To power their alien computer. **14** Spock chose to go into Starfleet rather than the Vulcan Science Academy. **15** *Friday's Child.* **16** Amanda Grayson. **17** Sybok. **18** By using power from the phasers. **19** A Sehlat with six-inch fangs. **20** Because the ship was crewed by Vulcans and Spock 'felt' their deaths. **21** Three. **22** T-negative (very rare). **23** T'Pring.

DOCTOR McCOY: PERSONAL LOG

1 Leonard Horatio McCoy. **2** Transporter. **3** Adrenaline. **4** Nancy. **5** Plum. **6** As "a simple country doctor". **7** By touching the tribal leader's wife. **8** A black knight. **9** Inject himself with cordrazine.

EPISODES

1 *Day Of The Dove.* **2** *The Naked Time.* **3** *The Paradise Syndrome.* **4** *Who Mourns For Adonais?* **5** *All Our Yesterdays.* **6** *Devil In The Dark.* **7** *The Enterprise Incident.* **8** *Friday's Child.* **9** *Mirror, Mirror.* **10** *Patterns Of Force.* **11** *This Side Of Paradise.* **12** *The Enemy Within.* **13** *The World Is Hollow And I Have Touched The Sky.* **14** *Wolf*

In The Fold. **15** *A Private Little War.* **16** *Mudd's Women.* **17** *Spectre Of The Gun.* **18** *The Cloud Miners.* **19** *The Savage Curtain.* **20** *Wink Of An Eye.* **21** *A Piece Of The Action.* **22** *Amok Time.* **23** *Let That Be Your Last Battlefield.* **24** *The Menagerie.* **25** *A Taste Of Armageddon.* **26** *The Menagerie.* **27** *Catspaw.* **28** *Metamorphosis.* **29** *Journey To Babel.* **30** *The Ultimate Computer.* **31** *Who Mourns For Adonais? and The Lights Of Zetar.* **32** *Turnabout Intruder.*

THE NEXT GENERATION
page 28

MULTIPLE CHOICE
1 b. **2** a. **3** c. **4** b. **5** b. **6** b. **7** b. **8** a. **9** b. **10** b. **11** c. **12** a. **13** a. **14** c. **15** b. **16** c. **17** c. **18** a.

THE CREW IN PERIL
1 Three Klingon warbird escorts decloak. **2** Nanites [microscopic robots]. **3** Dr. Pulaski. **4** They were caught in a causality loop. **5** Beverly Crusher. **6** By using the highly illegal phased cloaking device. **7** They disappear one by one until only Beverly is left. **8** By killing a member of the bridge crew. **9** By pointing a phaser at the dilithium chamber. **10** The Ferengi. **11** Because he has experience of theta band emissions. **12** Worf and Bev. **13** Bev Crusher and Picard. **14** An alien city. **15** There was too much synaptic damage. **16** It has a sweet smell. **17** Four. **18** A quantum filament. **19** *Descent II.* **20** Depressurising a shuttle bay. **21** Barclay's Protomorphosis Syndrome. **22** *Cause and Effect, Time Squared* and *Timescape.*

OBJECTS
1 Gold/yellow. **2** A hotel-cum-casino. **3** Misguided aliens took it to be an ideal example of human culture and built it out of guilt for lone astronaut Colonel Steven Richey after they accidentally killed the rest of his crew. **4** A glowing silver sphere. **5** A bio-chemical virus which can kill all life on a planet. **6** A walking stick with a serpent's head. **7** A drink. **8** The Custodian. **9** Exocomps. **10** Tricorder, Klingon, PADD, dagger, phaser. **11** A ceremonial mask representing the sun god, Masaka. **12** A deadly mitt, covered in poisonous spikes. **13** It has fifty-two stars. **14** It is a quantum phase inhibitor, capable of snuffing

out of the power of an entire star. **15** A statue given to Picard by Richard Galen in *The Chase.*

OBSERVATIONS

1 The Enterprise. **2** "Arch". **3** The various incarnations of the Enterprise. **4** One hundred and thirty seven. **5** Vulcans. **6** Cheap-looking worms. **7** Two. **8** Three times in *Encounter At Farpoint, Best Of Both Worlds II* and *Arsenal of Freedom.* **9** Five minutes. **10** U.S.S. Horatio. **11** 20%. **12** Two. **13** Junior. **14** 6 hours. **15** Klingon birds of prey. **16** A Midsummer Night's Dream. **17** Cholera. **18** 22 minutes. **19** 800 years. **20** *Measure Of A Man.* **21** *NCC 1305-E* or *NCC 71887.* **22** U.S.S. Victory. **23** At the Khitomer conference. **24** Leland T. Lynch. **25** Nine Times. **26** One. **27** U.S.S. Lantree. **28** 30,000. **29** Two years. **30** 20 years. **31** 17 days. **32** In the poker game and on the engineering monitors. **33** A lemur or pygmy marmoset. **34** Ginger tea with honey. **35** Steamed milk with nutmeg. **36** The Devron System, in the Klingon Neutral Zone.

THE ENTERPRISE CREW

1 Mr. Mott. **2** La Forge. **3** Riker. **4** Riker. **5** Riker. **6** Barclay. **7** They were exterminated by the Borg. **8** Natasha. **9** Picard. **10** Troi. **11** To rescue Troi. **12** Lwaxana, Deanna Troi, Riker. **13** Barclay's. **14** Beverly Crusher. **15** Geordi. **16** Worf. **17** Data, O'Brien, Troi. **18** Barclay. **19** Mr. Broccoli. **20** Picard and Data. **21** Picard, Ro, Guinan and Keiko. **22** Spock and Data. **23** A theatre company. **24** Samuel Clemens, aka Mark Twain. **25** Guinan. **26** Troi. **27** Picard and Beverly. **28** The ability to read each other's minds. **29** Riker. **30** Beverly's. **31** Ensign Ro. **32** By Armus, in *Skin of Evil.* **33** *The First Duty* and *Lower Decks.* **34** Killed on a secret mission in Cardassian Space. **35** By giving her a tongue-lashing about her academy history. **36** Data. **37** Fight to the death. **38** They fall into an underground cavern. **39** They buy it. **40** Geordi. **41** He asked for an adversary capable of 'defeating' Data. **42** Worf. **43** Guinan. **44** Riker. **45** Riker and Geordi. **46** Barclay. **47** Alien prisoners, removed from their bodies. **48** Riker and Data. **49** O'Brien. **50** Barclay. **51** Beverly Crusher. **52** Geordi and Ro. **53** Troi. **54** A spider. **55** Picard and Geordi. **56** American Indian culture. **57** Doctor Selar. **58** Three. **59** Five. **60** Gloria from Cleveland. **61** Geordi. **62** Because he is upset at not passing the Starfleet Entrance Exam. **63** Armus. **64** Eight. **65** Troi. **66** Because the planet has a steadfastly matriarchal society. **67** Because the planet is bathed in hyperonic radiation, usually lethal to humans. **68** Ensign Gomez.

69 McDuff. 70 Riker. 71 1200-1400. 72 Friar Tuck [Data], Robin Hood [Picard], Will Scarlet [Worf], Alan A'Dale [La Forge], Q [Sheriff of Nottingham], Vash [Maid Marian], and Riker [Little John]. 73 They project a false holographic rescue team. 74 It used a molecular decay detonator. 75 Worf's. 76 Troi. 77 REM sleep. 78 The piano. 79 In a Jeffries tube. 80 Tarellian Death Syndrome. 81 Worf. 82 Training for Starfleet's 'special forces'. 83 *The Child.*

CHARACTERS

1 James. 2 Inspector Lestrade. 3 The Romulan Sela. 4 He grows younger. 5 He supplied both sides in a civil war with weapons which prolonged the conflict for 40 years. 6 Kill him. 7 Admiral. 8 He committed suicide. 9 Deaf and dumb mediator. 10 Because he is a genetically engineered soldier. 11 A mud bath. 12 Ardra. 13 Temper. 14 Captain Picard. 15 Quark. 16 Guinan's. 17 By creating an illusionary Enterprise within the holodeck. 18 So she can destroy the Alliance's reactor. 19 To die. 20 Betazoid. 21 Because it had killed her son, Raymond. 22 An alien girl, Sarjenka. 23 Because he was 200 years old and unlikely to succumb to her charms. 24 Erase an entire species from existence. 25 Because he did not mention her to any of his crew. 26 In Sherwood Forest, in *Q-Pid*. 27 Ritual suicide ceremony. 28 Third of five. 29 He bought his way out. 30 Ishara Yar. 31 Mr. Zelo. 32 For having pornographic thoughts about her. 33 Nagilum. 34 Mistress Beata. 35 Tau Alpha C. 36 Dr. Kyla Marr. 37 Jenice Manheim. 38 The Ghorusda Disaster. 39 By being incredibly aggressive and abrupt [by being a Klingon basically]. 40 Barash. 41 Cook. 42 Timothy. 43 Data. 44 Because he believed he had caused it. 45 A human boy brought up as a Talarian. 46 By stabbing Picard. 47 Kivas Fajo. 48 Amanda Rogers. 49 By diverting a falling container. 50 Baran. 51 Pleasure, antagonism and love. 52 Eric Pressman.

PLOTS

1 The Ferengi. 2 Because they are all sterile. 3 On the holodeck. 4 Three. 5 *The Neutral Zone.* 6 Another Picard. 7 By 'possessing' Data. 8 In *Yesterday's Enterprise* she travelled back in time from an alternative timeline [it's confusing]. 9 Because he was a deaf mute. 10 It closed and they were lost 70,000 light years away. 11 The Delta quadrant. 12 On a cloaked Klingon ship. 13 To coach a growing underground movement of Unificationists. 14 The Vulcans. 15 They are genetically bred to perform tasks within their society. 16 By storing himself in the transport buffer. 17 By sending Hugh back as

an individual. **18** Data's head. **19** Aquiel's dog. **20** Three. **21** The Romulans, Klingons, and Cardassians. **22** Damage space. **23** By using the holodeck. **24** Their bases have been destroyed. **25** Three. **26** Fires gamma radiation into a computer they are inhabiting, killing a large number of them. **27** Details of a secret Romulan base in the Neutral Zone. **28** They are killed by a Solarian. **29** By teaching both sides sign language. **30** NCC-1701-C. **31** Because it is leaking deadly radiation. **32** Water. **33** To use her telepathic powers for profit. **34** They believed that it had some strategic significance and therefore could be turned into profit. **35** Dr. Nel Apgar himself. **36** By a bomb left over from an ancient war. **37** By creating a replica of his mother. **38** With a genetically engineered microvirus. **39** Destroys her with a phaser. **40** Lack of dreaming. **41** Because an argument over the love of a woman had started the war between the Krios and the Valt. **42** A human boy. **43** Three. **44** The three pips on Riker's collar – indicating that Riker's suggested course of action is best. **45** Sleep. **46** Because on a previous away mission they had been infected by alien DNA. **47** By making them wait for over an hour. **48** Trilithium Resin. **49** By defeating him in a fight. **50** The Romulans. **51** He commits suicide. **52** A rare plague vaccine. **53** Commander Remmick. **54** A housewife, a country and western singer, and a financier. **55** Felicium. **56** In a shuttle. **57** An explosion in the dilithium chamber. **58** By coding the information into his DNA. **59** By using his Betazoid powers of empathy. **60** 75 years. **61** They still believed the Klingons were at war with Starfleet. **62** An empathic metamorph. **63** A stellar core fragment. **64** He felt his race was not ready. **65** Hydrogen. **66** In a Klingon's forearm. **67** U.S.S. Phoenix. **68** Romulan spy. **69** A metagenic weapon. **70** To find one of their shuttles. **71** The Starfleet cadet. **72** By referring to a recent mission she could not have known about. **73** Because Troi senses deception in the captain. **74** Their transporter beam is diverted. **75** By resequencing his DNA.

CAPTAIN JEAN-LUC PICARD: PERSONAL LOG

1 Tea, Earl Grey, hot. **2** Admiral Nechayev. **3** The Stargazer. **4** Engaging warp and disengaging rapidly to give a ship the appearance of being in two places at once. **5** Dixon Hill. **6** San Francisco. **7** Right. **8** DaiMon Bok. **9** Attack the Enterprise with the Stargazer. **10** Artifical heart replacement. **11** Riker. **12** Locutus of Borg. **13** Four. **14** One of the Enterprise's shuttles. **15** To fetch his saddle. **16** Rock climbing. **17** He was rejected. **18** His entrance exam scores were good enough to get him another go. **19** He is stabbed in a bar fight with three Nausicaans. **20** *Tapestry*. **21** Picard had stood her up years before and they wanted to say goodbye properly. **22** A headache. **23** Because Lwaxana Troi is due on board. **24** Sexual prowess and readiness to take part in the sexual act. **25** Destroys it. **26** Chairman of the Atlantis Project. **27** By having a big scrap with him. **28** Because he's trapped in a transporter beam. **29** So he can be spirited away to an alien observation cell. **30** *Starship Mine*. **31** Q-Pid. **32** Because she is his wife. **33** By tapping it into Data's brain. **34** His artificial heart fails him. **35** She leaves the Enterprise. **36** LeBarre, France. **37** AF. **38** Organic chemistry. **39** He was the only first year student to win the marathon. **40** Dom-jot (an alien pool game).**41** Jack Crusher. **42** His mother. **43** Because they hibernate for six months out of every year. **44** Commandant of SFA. **45** By receiving an arrow in the chest. **46** A broken ankle. **47** Picard's Klingon knife. **48** A Christmas Carol. **49** Guinan. **50** Sings an old Academy drinking song. **51** Kamin. **52** Iron Weaver. **53** Gul Madred. **54** His daughter. **55** Lieutenant (junior grade) in astrophysics. **56** Lt. Commander Nella Daren (Stella Sciences).**57** He is suffering from Irumodic Syndrome.

FIRST OFFICER RIKER: PERSONAL LOG

1 Thomas. **2** On the holodeck. **3** A jazz bar. **4** By cheating. **5** Turns him off. **6** Risa. **7** 16 years. **8** The appearance of Minuet, his holodeck ideal women, as his wife. **9** His job. **10** Policeman. **11** The Pegasus. **12** Kyle. **13** Dr. Pulaski. **14** He gives Geordi his sight back, makes Wes a man, and gives Worf a mate. **15** Maggots. **16** *The Child*. **17** In a martial arts battle. **18** Murder. **19** By beating up the second officer. **20** Punches him to the ground. **21** 3D Chess. **22** Minuet. **23** Jean-Luc. **24** His arm. **25** Thomas. **26** Will Riker. **27** Stabbing somebody to death. **28** The Borg had won. **29** Eric Pressman. **30** Valdez, Alaska. **31** Three. **32** Aries, Drake, Melbourne. **33** Carmen Davila. **34** The Pagh. **35** Because the Judge Adjutant General's office is new and there are no staff to do the job. **36** Data's head. **37** He is caught in a riot and injured. **38** A phaser and a communicator. **39** Soren. **40** U.S.S. Potemkin. **41** A straw.

LT. COMMANDER DATA: PERSONAL LOG

1 Dr. Noonian Soong. **2** Left. **3** Yellow. **4** Geordi. **5** At the base of his spine. **6** Positronic. **7** Tasha Yar. **8** Hostility. **9** Ode To Spot. **10** Lore. **11** Sela. **12** Spot. **13** Ginger. **14** TRICK QUESTION. Spot is male throughout the series until *Genesis* when the cat mysteriously becomes female. **15** To give him an emotion chip. **16** His emotion chip. **17** Q. **18** By flashing a hand torch into their eyes. **19** By playing poker. **20** *Descent I.* **21** Anger. **22** An android. **23** No. **24** Omicron Theta. **25** Run around naked. **26** Two. Tasha Yar and Ensign Jenna D'Sora. **27** NFN stands for No First Name, while NMI means No Middle Initial. **28** Operations Manager [or 'ops]. **29** The Schizoid Man. **30** A stand-up comedy routine. **31** Ira Graves. **32** A medal given to him by Picard and a picture of Tasha Yar. **33** Lal. **34** Hindi. **35** Beloved. **36** She could use contractions and experience motions. **37** Riker. **38** By threatening to kill his assistant. **39** Because Picard told him to. **40** The first officer. **41** Because Data is an android. **42** Six. **43** Himself, the bad guy Frank Hollander, his son Eli, and the two henchmen, and a prostitute. **44** To test the theory: 'a watched pot never boils'. **45** That Spot's kittens are not affected by the virus. **46** *Phantasms.* **47** Four. **48** Julianna Soong. **49** 100 kg. **50** 74. **51** *In Theory.* **52** *The Outrageous Okona.* **53** 21 years. **54** The middle one. **55** 4 days. **56** *The Schizoid Man.* **57** Strategema. **58** A bunny rabbit. **59** By resigning from Starfleet. **60** The bartender. **61** Because he is standing behind the bar when the memory loss occurs. **62** The Model T of androids. **63** Bar job in Ten Forward. **64** U.S.S. Sutherland. **65** An acrylic scuplture. **66** Plasma discharge from a field generator. **67** A blacksmith. **68** Pleasure. **69** Geordi. **70** 411. **71** An old-fashioned telephone. **72** The very real infestation of the ship by interphasic insects. **73** Let out a high-pitched shriek. **74** Prospero from *The Tempest.*

LIEUTENANT WORF: PERSONAL LOG

1 Alexander. **2** Holodeck. **3** K'Ehleyr. **4** Klingon Ambassador. **5** Inside a Class 8 probe. **6** Duras. **7** Kurn. **8** Because his father is wrongly accused of being a traitor. **9** His blood. **10** No. **11** A broken spine. **12** A container falls on him. **13** By recreating it on the holodeck. **14** Riker. **15** Alexander from the future. **16** Worf's half-brother. **17** Mogh. **18** At the Battle of Khitomer. **19** Dr. Pulaski. **20** Scrambled eggs. **21** Kurn takes Riker's place on board the Enterprise in an exchange thing. **22** Because of his discommendation. **23** *Redemption I.* **24** Troi. **25** By challenging him to do so. **26** By fashioning a force field from his communicator. **27** His new photon configuration. **28** False. It is all part of an empathic vision Troi has. **29** He is, of course, the first Klingon to have served in Starfleet. **30** His nursemaid [or Ghajmok]. **31** By killing him. **32** A poisoned tea ceremony. **33** Ice-man. **34** Projects an image of a Romulan warbird on the viewscreen. **35** *Hide and Q* and *Transfigurations.* **36** Six years. **37** It was part of the ceremony to regain his family's honour. **38** Weapon's officer. **39** After Worf broke his back in *Ethics.* **40** Stealing a model

dinosaur. **41** A Klingon spear. **42** Accidentally cuts his forehead.
43 Telling Alex about the Rite of Ascension.

COMMANDER GEORDI LA FORGE: PERSONAL LOG

1 Chief Engineer. **2** He is kidnapped and brainwashed by the
Romulans. **3** Data. **4** He would have been killed at birth for his
blindness. **5** All his life. **6** His mother. **7** He didn't – he was born
blind. **8** Twice. **9** Dizziness. **10** *Booby Trap*. **11** Leah Brahms.
12 The Hera. **13** He's an exozoologist. **14** First Officer. **15** U.S.S.
Brittain. **16** Ensign Tyler.

COUNSELLOR TROI: PERSONAL LOG

1 Riker. **2** 7 years. **3** Lwaxana. **4** Mr. Homn. **5** *Haven*. **6** Chocolate.
7 By ordering Geordi to his death to save the ship. **8** *The Child*. **9** Her
empathic abilities. **10** That Troi had a sister who died at a young age.
11 An amphibian. **12** Psychology. **13** She ages rapidly and becomes
incredibly possessive and is inexplicably dressed in a diaphanous
dress. **14** Because she is being used as a receptacle for all of Alkar's
negative emotions. **15** Goddess of Empathy. **16** A cellular peptide
cake. **17** Ro, and Chief O'Brien. **18** She resigns. **19** By filling her
head with a repetitive tune. **20** That she wear a standard uniform.
21 A blotted-out memory of her daughter's death. **22** Ian Andrew.
23 Ian Andrew Troi. **24** Kestra. **25** Kaferian Apples. **26** 36 hours.
27 Wyatt Miller. **28** That they are assassins. **29** Rai. **30** She was
being controlled by the Paxans. **31** Major.

DOCTOR BEVERLY CRUSHER: PERSONAL LOG

1 Dance. **2** Nurse Ogawa. **3** Odan is a trill and his new host is a
woman. **4** In their heirloom, a candle. **5** Because Ronin (the rather
sexual lifeform) has 'convinced' her to stay. **6** Head of Starfleet
Medical. **7** Howard. **8** Dancing. **9** John Doe. **10** She gets trapped in
a warp bubble. **11** The Traveller. **12** Because he ordered her not to.
z**13** Because a Ferengi body should not be touched before funeral
ceremonies. **14** Copernicus City, Luna. **15** Attempting to jettison a
damaged warp nacelle on the U.S.S. Stargazer. **16** Picard decided he
would be killed if he tried to rescue Jack so saved other crew
members instead. **17** Wesley Crusher. **18** Bev's mentor and friend in
Remember Me. **19** *Cyrano De Bergerac*, *The Pirates Of Penzance*,
Frame Of Mind. **20** Felisia Howard. **21** Ronin. **22** U.S.S. Pasteur.

ENSIGN WESLEY CRUSHER: PERSONAL LOG

1 Jack Crusher. **2** The Traveller. **3** He fails [ha-ha]. **4** His father. **5** American Indians. **6** Grey. **7** *The Naked Now*. **8** Falling on some flowers. **9** Lethal injection. **10** A precocious fifteen. **11** Another human, a Vulcan, and a Benzite. **12** *Final Mission*. **13** The shuttle craft crashes on a desert planet. **14** His father's death. **15** Nova squadron. **16** Fourteen. **17** Lieutenant Commander. **18** Kolvord Starburst. **19** Robin Lefler. **20** Mozart [For God's Sake!] **21** *Ménage A Troi*.

ENSIGN RO: PERSONAL LOG

1 Bajoran [if you got this one wrong you should just give up]. **2** That she has died. **3** Laren. **4** Wrinkled nose, and a dangly earring in the right ear. **5** Con. **6** Riker. **7** *Conundrum*. **8** U.S.S. Wellington. **9** She was court martialled and imprisoned. **10** Separate the saucer section and get away. **11** She disobeyed orders on an away mission and, as a result, eight people died.

Q: PERSONAL LOG

1 Froze him solid. **2** 24 hours. **3** Join the Q, or become human and never display her powers again. **4** A really good laugh. **5** The Q Continuum. **6** Eight. **7** *Hide And Q, Q-Who?, Q-Pid, All Good Things, Deja-Q, Encounter At Farpoint, Tapestry, True-Q*. **8** Worf and Wes. **9** By selflessly leaving the Enterprise so the Calamarain will just destroy him. **10** Four. **11** A French Marshal's uniform. **12** God of Lies. **13** 2005. **14** A tornado.

EPISODES

1 *Timescape*. **2** *Eye Of The Beholder, Parallels, All Good Things. . . .* **3** *Disaster, Face Of The Enemy, Thine Own Self*. **4** *The Pegasus, The Next Phase*. **5** *Lessons*. **6** *Schisms*. **7** *Descent II* and *Suspicions*. **8** *The Battle*. **9** *The Icarus Factor*. **10** *Face Of The Enemy*. **11** *The Enemy*. **12** *The Most Toys*. **13** *Chain of Command*. **14** *Arsenal Of Freedom, Encounter At Farpoint*, and *Best Of Both Worlds II*. **15** *Measure of A Man*. **16** *The Battle*. **17** *The Host*. **18** *The Naked Now*. **19** *Journey's End*. **20** *Inheritance*. **21** *Nth Degree*. **22** *Schisms*. **23** *Pre-Emptive Strike*. **24** *Emissary*. **25** *Contagion*. **26** *Galaxy's Child*. **27** *Q-Who?* **28** *Conundrum* and *The Emissary*. **29** *Time's Arrow 1*. **30** *All Good Things*. **31** *Hide and Q, Loud As A Whisper*. **32** *Disaster*. **33** *A Matter Of Honour*. **34** *Who Watches The Watchers?* **35** *The Child*. **36** *Ménage A Troi*. **37** *Sarek*. **38** *Sins Of*

The Father. **39** *The Mind's Eye.* **40** *The Naked Now.* **41** *Haven.*
42 *Disaster.* **43** *The Child.* **44** *Tapestry.* **45** *Angel One.*
46 *Requiem For Methuselah.* **47** *Conundrum.* **48** *Cardassians.*
49 *Relics.* **50** *All Good Things…*

DEEP SPACE   page 72

MULTIPLE CHOICE
1 b. **2** b. **3** a. **4** b. **5** a. **6** c. **7** b. **8** a. **9** a. **10** a. **11** b. **12** c.

CREW
1 Dr. Bashir's. **2** O'Brien. **3** Sisko, Kira, Dax and Bashir. **4** Bashir.
5 Sisko's. **6** O'Brien (or rather his clone). **7** Kira. **8** A dream. **9** Kira.
10 She rescued prisoners of war from a Cardassian prison planet.
11 Commander Sisko and Lt. Dax. **12** Bajoran versus Federation.
13 Dax. **14** Sisko, Kira, Bashir. **15** Psychokinetic abilities.
16 O'Brien. **17** Because they know about the virus. **18** By taking a
drink. **19** Odo. **20** Hopscotch. **21** Because he suffered from Kalla
Nohro Syndrome only suffered by those present at a certain Bajoran
labour camp. Oh, and he had cosmetically altered his appearance to
look like the dreaded Gul. **22** A proto-universe.

CHARACTERS
1 Quark. **2** Garak. **3** Tailor and clothes shop owner. **4** He dies. **5** Q
took her there. **6** Kai Opaka. She is killed, but then resurrected by
airborne nano-viruses. **7** Keiko's. **8** Because the gravity on her planet
is much less than on Earth. **9** Tosk. **10** Morn. **11** Odo. **12** Pup.
13 Selling explosives to a militant Bajoran terrorist group. **14** Vedek
Winn. **15** Hid under the table and wept. **16** The aged Klingon trio in
Blood Oath. **17** Because Croden killed his twin Ah-Kel. **18** One million
bars of gold-pressed latinum. **19** Apprentice engineer. **20** He's
stabbed by a Bajoran just for being Cardassian. **21** Mullibok.
22 Vorad. **23** Tosk. **24** To be pursued and to give a good challenge
for his pursuers. **25** Self-sealing stem bolts. **26** An area of land on
Bajor. **27** Commander Hudson.

PLOTS

1 Speaking gibberish. **2** The thoughts of the villagers. **3** Vedek Bareil. **4** Vedek Winn. **5** *The Circle*. **6** Dax's symbiont. **7** Bajor. **8** Technology. **9** A defensive satellite system. **10** In the food replicators. **11** The Bajoran underground during the war. **12** His daughter, Yareth. **13** In a holosuite. **14** Because he cloned himself and then killed the clone. **15** An alien lifeform (surprise, surprise). **16** Close up the wormhole. **17** So Bajor won't be tainted by either Federation or Cardassian presence. **18** Duridium. **19** A latinum brooch. **20** In one of Quark's holosuites. **21** On a Vulcan science vessel. **22** By installing a circuit breaker in Security.

POT POURRI

1 A comet. **2** Via a stable wormhole. **3** The creature which hosts a Trill's body. **4** The Dominion. **5** The Founders. **6** The Jem'hadar. **7** Quark and Dr. Bashir. **8** Linear time. **9** The U.S.S. Defiant. **10** It was built to beat the Borg. **11** Elevated neutrino readings. **12** Buck Bokai. **13** To make a solid colour using the theta waves of your brain.

COMMANDER SISKO: PERSONAL LOG

1 Benjamin. **2** Jake. **3** Baseball. **4** Yes, in *Emissary*. **5** Emissary. **6** In the battle with the Borg at Wolf 359. **7** Jennifer. **8** Benjy. **9** A loveable rogue (or pirate if you like). **10** Three years. **11** U.S.S. Saratoga. **12** In the Utopia Planetia Shipyards, Mars. **13** By threatening to imprison his nephew Nog. **14** Aubergine stew.

MAJOR KIRA: PERSONAL LOG

1 The Bajoran Underground. **2** A prostitute. **3** Vedek Bareil. **4** Bajoran Liaison. **5** *The Circle*. **6** *The Circle*. **7** By burning down his house. **8** Her job. **9** Lee Nullas. **10** They described her as a "minor terrorist".

LIEUTENANT DAX: PERSONAL LOG

1 Trill. **2** Commander Sisko. **3** Old man. **4** Curzon. **5** Another Trill, Vorad, attempts to steal her symbiont. **6** Because he was in bed with the General's wife at the time. **7** 80 years ago. **8** Three times. **9** Once. **10** General Ardelon Tando. **11** 93 hours. **12** 440 years.

CHIEF O'BRIEN: PERSONAL LOG

1 Miles Edward. **2** Data. **3** The Cardassians. **4** Ten Forward. **5** On holiday. **6** Molly. **7** Rumplestiltskin. **8** Worf. **9** The Cardies. **10** A back tooth. **11** Number three. **12** Two. **13** The Sirah's apprentice, Hovath. **14** Spiders.

ODO: PERSONAL LOG

1 A bucket. **2** Because he can only approximate the complex appearance of human beings. **3** Lwaxana Troi. **4** Constable. **5** Every 16 hours. **6** A pendant key which changes shape. **7** 'Be the life of the party' and change into any object his audience wanted. **8** He was the Bajoran scientist assigned to examine Odo. **9** He is the slave-master. **10** On the Denorios asteroid belt near DS9. **11** Aside from the fact that Odo sent Ibudan to gaol sometime in the past, the holosuite was locked from the inside. **12** They force him to enter a small container and then place it in a stasis chamber. **13** *The Passenger*.

QUARK: PERSONAL LOG

1 Rom. **2** Nog. **3** Dabo. **4** Because he cheated them at Dabo. **5** His brother sells his seat. **6** A 'promotion' plus a free drink. **7** A list of Bajoran collaborators. **8** Barbo. **9** Betrayed him to the authorities for profit. **10** Quark's brother, Rom. **11** Chula.

BAJORAN CULTURE AND HISTORY

1 Your inner spirit or soul. **2** The Kai. **3** A Bajoran freedom/terrorist group. **4** The Celestial Temple. **5** The Prophets. **6** Nine. **7** The Cardassians. **8** 10,000. **9** An underground resistance movement. **10** The Gratitude Festival. **11** Bajoran edible spiders. **12** 60 years. **13** Minister Jarrow Rasa.

FERENGI CULTURE AND HISTORY

1 The Rules of Acquisition. **2** The Grand Nagus. **3** Nothing. **4** On their ears. **5** Zek. **6** Profit. **7** Family. **8** DaiMon. **9** 285. **10** Mother. **11** Friendship. **12** Sexual prowess. **13** Caress his ears.

CARDASSIAN CULTURE AND HISTORY

1 Gul. **2** Gul Dukat. .**3** A notorious sadistic Cardassian occupier. **4** Guilty. **5** Terek Nor. **6** Drink it.

DEEP SPACE NINE HISTORY AND SPECIFICATIONS

1 The Promenade. **2** Elliptical. **3** Keiko O'Brien. **4** Gold-pressed latinum. **5** Holosuites. **6** Inverted vest colours. **7** Ops. **8** Rio Grande, Ganges, Yangtze Kiang. **9** Living quarters. **10** The infirmary. **11** 18 years. **12** 7000. **13** 300. **14** Isolinear rods. **15** The Cardassians had wrecked it before leaving.

EPISODES

1 *Emissary*. **2** *Battle Lines*. **3** *Q-Less*. **4** *Dax*. **5** *Crossover*. **6** *A Man Alone*. **7** *The Storyteller*. **8** *The Nagus*. **9** *Blood Oath*. **10** *Rules Of Acquisition*. **11** *The Homecoming, The Circle, The Siege*. **12** *Past Prologue*. **13** *Past Prologue*. **14** *Vortex*.

THE FILMS
page 90

I: THE MOTION PICTURE

1 Admiral. **2** Kirk. **3** Willard Decker. **4** *The Doomsday Machine*. **5** Lieutenant. **6** The Maker. **7** Carbon-based units. **8** A meteor. **9** Because he senses the mind of the alien probe. **10** He leaves the ship in a space suit and mind melds with the probe. **11** Ilia. **12** Navigation. **13** The Voyager space probe. **14** He becomes part of V'ger.

II: THE WRATH OF KHAN

1 Fifty two years old. **2** Romulan Ale, Spectacles, *A Tale Of Two Cities*. **3** McCoy, Spock, Scotty, Sulu and Uhura. **4** The unwinnable SFA simulation. **5** Kirk. **6** By reprogramming the simulator. **7** Vulcan. **8** Botany Bay. **9** Khan Noonian Singh. **10** Marla McGivers. **11** Ship's historian. **12** Parasitic sand creature. **13** Neighbouring planet Ceti Alpha IV exploded, altering V's orbit. **14** U.S.S. Reliant. **15** Regula 1. **16** Carol Marcus. **17** She was an old flame. **18** David Marcus. **19** One day. **20** By turning the phaser on himself. **21** By transmitting the ship's prefix code. **22** "by the book". **23** A Starfleet badge. **24** 300. **25** By getting the main power on line. **26** Mutara Nebula. **27** Spock. **28** A photon-torpedo casing.

III: THE SEARCH FOR SPOCK

1 Sarek. **2** Placed his 'katra' inside him before he died. **3** By watching video records of the event. **4** They steal it. **5** It carries the first 'transwarp' drive. **6** NX-2000. **7** Because Scotty has sabotaged the engines. **8** Kruge. **9** U.S.S. Grissom. **10** Because it only has a skeleton crew. **11** Stabbed by a Klingon Warrior, trying to save Saavik. **12** Self-destructs it. **13** T'Lar. **14** T'Pau. **15** Jim Kirk. **16** It becomes unstable and blows up.

IV: THE VOYAGE HOME

1 Sarek. **2** The Bounty. **3** Three. **4** How do you feel? **5** Saavik. **6** By ionising the atmosphere. **7** Humpback. **8** By slingshotting around the sun's gravity well. **9** *Tomorrow Is Yesterday.* **10** San Francisco. **11** Refuse collectors (dustmen). **12** Wears a headband. **13** A punk. **14** Because his music was too loud. **15** Dr. Gillian Taylor. **16** George and Gracie. **17** She tells him. **18** Helicopter. **19** Chekov and Uhura. **20** To avoid publicity. **21** Chekov. **22** Injecting high energy neutrons. **23** By using the transporter. **24** He guesses. **25** Nine. **26** Demotion to captain.

V: THE FINAL FRONTIER

1 Yosemite National Park. **2** Planet of Galactic Peace. **3** Paradise City. **4** Humans, Romulans, Klingons. **5** Half-brother. **6** The quest for ultimate knowledge. **7** Touching them, or using his telepathic abilities to make them face their worse fears. **8** The death of his father. **9** He switched off his life support just days before a cure was found. **10** His birth and Sarek's unhappiness with it. **11** Because "he needs his pain". **12** The Great Barrier. **13** Copernicus. **14** Their ship. **15** Sybok's. **16** 'Row, row, row your boat'.

VI: THE UNDISCOVERED COUNTRY

1 The Future. **2** Praxis. **3** U.S.S. Excelsior. **4** Fifty years. **5** Because they killed his son. **6** Chancellor Gorkon. **7** General Chang. **8** Kronos One. **9** A ship that can fire when cloaked. **10** Two. **11** Assassination of a member of the High Council. **12** Rura Penthe or "aliens' graveyard". **13** A shapeshifter. **14** Martia. **15** His daughter, Azetbur. **16** By mind melding with her. **17** Camp Khitomer. **18** Shakespeare. **19** Gravity boots. **20** The kitchens.

GENERATIONS

1 Sulu, Uhura and Spock. **2** The Enterprise B. **3** Guinan. **4** Lieutenant Commander. **5** His nephew and brother. **6** In a fire, back on Earth. **7** His emotion chip. **8** Geordi. **9** By destroying entire stars to direct it. **10** Lursa and B'Etor. **11** A Christmas tree ornament. **12** On a farm in Iowa. **13** It crashes and is destroyed.

POT POURRI

1 Two. **2** Kirstie Alley. **3** Iman. **4** Michael Dorn [aka Worf]. **5** His great great grandfather. **6** Christopher Plummer. **7** ST VI: *The Undiscovered Country*. On the video version only apparently. **8** His wife. **9** Isaac Asimov. **10** ST III. **11** ST III. **12** 27 years. **13** ST V: *The Final Frontier*. **14** An old man with white hair and a very droopy moustache [Santa Claus is a valid answer]. **15** Whoopi Goldberg.

THE ALIENS *page 100*

MULTIPLE CHOICE

1 b. **2** b. **3** b. **4** b. **5** c. **6** a. **7** a. **8** b. **9** a. **10** c. **11** a. **12** c.

VULCAN HISTORY AND CULTURE

1 Logic. **2** Green. **3** The Vulcan coming-of-age ceremony. **4** The Vulcan 'life force'. **5** Because he lusts for blood [plak tow = blood fever]. **6** A pet [with six-inch fangs]. **7** Princess. **8** 'S'. **9** 'T'. **10** Vulcan secret security. **11** To rid their minds of all emotions. **12** Mind meld. **13** The Home of God. **14** Leather nooses. **15** A spade with a heavy knob on the end. **16** The ceremony for uniting a Vulcan's spirit with a living body. **17** Surak. **18** He guided his people from emotionalism to logic. **19** Bendii Syndrome. **20** An ancient telepathic weapon. **21** Copper based. **22** Infinite Diversity in Infinite Combinations.

KLINGON HISTORY AND CULTURE

1 For backup, in case of failure. **2** Bluff. **3** His entire family. **4** A figure in Klingon mythology. **5** He united the Klingon Empire under single rule. **6** The main weapon of a Klingon warrior. **7** Fire! **8** You will be killed [for it is an insult]. **9** A plate of live worms. **10** The Duras sisters. **11** Lursa and B'Etor. **12** The Romulans. **13** Gowron. **14** Worf. **15** Assassinate him. **16** From the Romulans. **17** Peacemaker. **18** K'Plah. **19** They don't have tear ducts.

20 Purple. 21 The traditional knife of a Klingon warrior. 22 A pet. 23 The Klingon bonding ceremony [marriage]. 24 The Rite of Succession. 25 Recite all the battles and prizes he has won as a warrior to prove his worth. 26 Having sex. 27 Korris, Konnel, Kunivas. 28 A delicacy. 29 Commit ritual suicide. 30 Arbiter of Succession. 31 Toral. 32 Excommunication from the Klingon Empire. 33 They are dishonoured. 34 They walk between two ranks of Klingons who stab them with painsticks. 35 Kahless's. 36 Kronos [Kling is also acceptable]. 37 First City. 38 Kahless's brother. 39 Kahless, lock of his hair, in a volcanic stream. 40 A god. 41 An opera. 42 A Klingon spear. 43 Heaven. 44 Devil. 45 His champion. 46 Drink it. 47 Sword of Honour. 48 Ten generations. 49 Fifteen. 50 K'Mpec. 51 He was poisoned. 52 Ja'Rod, father of Duras.

BETAZOID HISTORY AND CULTURE
1 Nothing. 2 True. Troi is half-human. 3 Ferengi. 4 Vash. 5 Tapping two fingers behind the ear. 6 Betazoid women go sex mad in menopause. 7 By banging a gong. 8 Genetically. 9 Childhood. 10 The fifth house.

ROMULAN HISTORY AND CULTURE
1 Tasha Yar's. 2 Blue. 3 The Klingons. 4 Two. 5 The Beta Quadrant. 6 "Jolan Tru". 7 An artificial quantum singularity. 8 An artificial black hole. 9 The Romulan secret police. 10 Heaven.

POT POURRI
1 Weaponry. 2 Tourism. 3 Portal. 4 Deneb IV. 5 Romulans [and Klingons]. 6 O and 1. 7 Quadrotricale [wheat]. 8 Humans [according to the crystalline life-form in *Home Soil.* 9 Three hundred and seventy two. 10 The Cardassians.

ALIENS: TRUE OR FALSE?
1 True. 2 True. 3 False [Turkana 4]. 4 True. 5 False [He was an omnipotent Douwd]. 6 True. 7 False [They used metaphor]. 8 False [They use binary which is Base 2]. 9 True. 10 False [It was called Armus]. 11 True. 12 True. 13 True. 14 False [They are telepathic]. 15 False [They eat wheat].16 False [They hate Klingons]. 17 True. 18 True. 19 False [They all carry a genetic plague virus]. 20 False [The Cardassians were peaceful until the military took over]. 21 True. 22 True. 23 True. 24 True. 25 True. 26 True. 27 False [They can assume any shape]. 28 True. 29 True. 30 False [It was described as

'incomprehensible'). **31** True. **32** True. **33** True. **34** False (They were wiped out by neural parasites). **35** True. **36** False (They were descended from Irish farmers). **37** True. **38** True. **39** False (Bajoran society is thousands of years older than Earth's). **40** False ("It's green"). **41** True. **42** False (The Grisellans do). **43** True. **44** True. **45** False (They are insectoid). **46** True. **47** True. **48** False (They don't have paws). **49** False (It looks like a snowflake). **50** True.

BEHIND THE SCENES
page 114

ACTORS' NAMES

1 Patrick Stewart. **2** Jonathan Frakes. **3** Brent Spiner. **4** Avery Brooks. **5** Gates McFadden. **6** Marina Sirtis. **7** LeVar Burton. **8** Michael Dorn. **9** Wil Wheaton. **10** Majel Barrett. **11** Colm Meaney. **12** Whoopi Goldberg. **13** James Doohan. **14** William Shatner. **15** Leonard Nimoy. **16** DeForest Kelly. **17** George Takei. **18** Nana Visitor. **19** Denise Crosby. **20** Terry Farrell. **21** Siddig El Fadil. **22** Rene Auberjonois. **23** Armin Shimerman. **24** John de Lancie. **25** Walter Koenig. **26** Dianna Muldaur. **27** Nichelle Nichols. **28** Dwight Schultz. **29** Louise Fletcher. **30** Philip Anglim. **31** Aron Eisenberg. **32** Max Grodenchik. **33** Rosaline Chao. **34** Michelle Forbes. **35** Cirroc Lofton. **36** Carel Struycken. **37** Patti Yasutake. **38** Grace Lee Whitney. **39** Brian Bonsall and Jon Steuer. **40** Camille Saviola.

GUEST STARS

1 Professor Stephen Hawking. **2** *Descent I.* **3** Joan Collins. **4** Nurse Chapel. **5** The computer voice. **6** Charles Bronson. **7** Q2. **8** David Soul. **9** *The A-Team.* **10** Howling Mad Murdoch. **11** *Guys And Dolls.* **12** The evil Klingon Cpt. Kruge. **13** *The Colbys.* **14** He played Kalin/Picard's son. **15** *A Matter Of Time.* **16** *The Addams Family.* **17** *The Dauphin.* **18** *Twin Peaks.* **19** Stephanie Beacham. **20** *Robocop* and *Total Recall.* **21** *Manhunt.* **22** *Darmok.* **23** Captain Bateman in *Cause And Effect.* **24** Vedeik Winn. **25** Steven Spielberg (for he is David Spielberg). **26** *Balance Of Terror.* **27** ST I. **28** The Mommas And The Papas. **29** She played Dava, Timcin's daughter, in *Half A Life.* **30** The Sicilian.

ACTORS' LIVES

1 Bing Crosby. **2** *A Christmas Carol.* **3** *The Commitments.* **4** *The Snapper.* **5** *T.J. Hooker.* **6** *Mission: Impossible.* **7** Yeoman Janice Rand. **8** Two. **9** *Stand By Me.* **10** *Excalibur.* **11** *Hellraiser III.* **12** Under Siege. **13** *Genesis.* **14** *Three Men And A Baby.* **15** *Airplane II: The Sequel.* **16** Walter Koenig. **17** *Dead Ringers.* **18** *First Contact.* **19** *The Wicked Lady.* **20** *The Last Outpost.* **21** *Kalifornia.* **22** *Benson.* **23** LeVar Burton. **24** *Attached, Cause And Effect, The Chase, The Offspring, Sub Rosa.* **25** *The Pegasus* and *Second Chances.* **26** *Robin Hood: Men In Tights.* **27** The middle finger of his right hand. [You didn't know that did you?] They film him very cleverly and use stand-ins when we need to see both hands, but if you watch ST V very carefully you can see his missing digit.] **28** *Spenser: For Hire.* **29** The rather tough Hawk. **30** *Fistful of Datas, In Theory, Hero Worship.*

POT POURRI

1 ST I. **2** Spock [he was in the pilot, *The Cage*]. **3** A Jewish ritual. **4** George La Forge, an ST fan who died of musculary dystrophy in 1975. **5** *The Cage.* **6** Leonard Nimoy [Spock] and Majel Barrett [Number 1]. **7** 178. **8** 79. **9** 19. **10** The Maquis. **11** He's a holodeck simulation. **12** Patrick Stewart, Jonathan Frakes, LeVar Burton, Michael Dorn, Gates McFadden, Marina Sirtis, Brent Spiner. **13** Wesley Crusher. **14** Helm. **15** Robert Bloch, author of *Psycho.* **16** The third season. **17** *Hero Worship.* **18** Twenty-six. **19** James Doohan. **20** Techno-babble. **21** "Space. . .the final frontier. . .these are the voyages of the Starship Enterprise. Its five year mission: to seek out new life and new civilisations, to seek out strange new worlds. . . to boldly go where no man has gone before. . ." **22** "Space. . . .the final frontier. . .these are the voyages of the Starship Enterprise. Its continuing mission: to seek out new life, and new civilisations. . . to boldly go where no one has gone before. . ." **23** Gene Roddenberry. **24** Michael Piller. **25** Rick Berman.

BEHIND THE SCENES: TRUE OR FALSE?

1 True. **2** True. **3** True. **4** True. **5** True. **6** True. **7** False. **8** True. **9** True. **10** True. **11** True. **12** True. **13** True. **14** True. **15** True.

SEEN EVERY EPISODE?

SEASON ONE
1 i. **2** d. **3** k. **4** u. **5** q. **6** e. **7** a. **8** y. **9** m. **10** o. **11** s. **12** x. **13** f. **14** b. **15** v. **16** n. **17** g. **18** l. **19** c. **20** h. **21** r. **22** w. **23** j. **24** p. **25** t.

SEASON TWO
1 h. **2** a. **3** l. **4** j. **5** r. **6** e. **7** q. **8** v. **9** b. **10** d. **11** n. **12** s. **13** t. **14** o. **15** f. **16** g. **17** c. **18** m. **19** k. **20** i. **21** p. **22** u.

SEASON THREE
1 y. **2** m. **3** g. **4** d. **5** a. **6** i. **7** o. **8** r. **9** u. **10** e. **11** b. **12** t. **13** j. **14** w. **15** x. **16** z. **17** h. **18** c. **19** f. **20** k. **21** q. **22** l. **23** p. **24** s. **25** n. **26** v.

SEASON FOUR
1 b. **2** m. **3** g. **4** s. **5** x. **6** i. **7** c. **8** z. **9** w. **10** j. **11** p. **12** l. **13** d. **14** y. **15** h. **16** e. **17** o. **18** r. **19** v. **20** k. **21** q. **22** f. **23** n. **24** t. **25** a. **26** u.

SEASON FIVE
1 i. **2** g. **3** c. **4** k. **5** z. **6** x. **7** b. **8** e. **9** n. **10** p. **11** u. **12** s. **13** m. **14** j. **15** a. **16** w. **17** l. **18** r. **19** f. **20** d. **21** h. **22** o. **23** q. **24** t. **25** v. **26** y.

SEASON SIX
1 p. **2** o. **3** v. **4** i. **5** c. **6** a. **7** g. **8** l. **9** q. **10** r. **11** x. **12** z. **13** j. **14** f. **15** h. **16** u. **17** y. **18** t. **19** m. **20** n. **21** k. **22** e. **23** b. **24** d. **25** s. **26** w.

SEASON SEVEN
1 p. **2** n. **3** v. **4** g. **5** s. **6** j. **7** b. **8** u. **9** o. **10** a. **11** l. **12** k. **13** c. **14** m. **15** y. **16** r. **17** e. **18** d. **19** q. **20** t. **21** x. **22** h. **23** i. **24** f. **25** w.

QUOTES

1 WHO: Riker to Worf. EPISODE: *Parallels.* CONTEXT: Worf suspects [with some dread] that he is to be the 'victim' of a surprise birthday party on returning to the Enterprise after a combat tournament.

2 WHO: Riker to Data. EPISODE: *Frame Of Mind.* CONTEXT: Riker is somewhat unhappy about his imaginary [or is it?] stay in an alien mental asylum.

3 WHO: Worf. EPISODE: *Q-Pid.* CONTEXT: Worf is not pleased that he has been turned into one of Robin Hood's henchmen by Q.

4 WHO: McCoy. EPISODE: *The Enemy Within.* CONTEXT: McCoy sums up the biological state of a recently transported 'space dog' to Captain Kirk.

5 WHO: Worf to Wesley. EPISODE: *The Dauphin.* CONTEXT: Worf is explaining the subtleties of Klingon courtship to a naive Crusher boy.

6 WHO: Worf to the Uxbridges. EPISODE: *The Survivors.* CONTEXT: Worf is, as ever, ill at ease with the human necessity for small talk.

7 WHO: K'Ehleyr to Worf. EPISODE: *Reunion.* CONTEXT: K'Ehleyr tries to engage a stoic Worf in romantic thoughts.

8 WHO: Data to the assembled crew members. EPISODE: *Schisms.* CONTEXT: Data is performing a less than emotionally rousing poem called 'Ode to Spot' to the bored crew.

9 WHO: Data to collected dinner guests [including Lwaxana and Deanna Troi] EPISODE: *The Haven.* CONTEXT: A celebratory meal isn't going down too well.

10 WHO: Q to Worf. EPISODE: *Hide And Q.* CONTEXT: Worf asks Picard's persmission to attack Q. Picard refuses and Q is indignant.

11 WHO: Eline [Picard's wife] to Picard. EPISODE: *The Inner Light.* CONTEXT: Struck by an alien probe, Picard has just lived an entire lifetime in 22 minutes. At the end of his 'life', his long dead friends rise to greet him and explain what has happened.

12 WHO: Picard to Riker. EPISODE: *The Pegasus*. CONTEXT: Picard is very unhappy at being kept in the dark about the Pegasus.

13 WHO: Picard to courtroom. EPISODE: *Measure Of A Man*. CONTEXT: Picard sums up his defense of Data as a sentient being.

14 WHO: Moriarty to Pulaski. EPISODE: *Elementary, My Dear Data*. CONTEXT: Moriarty has been holding Pulaski hostage on the holodeck and fondly remembers the time when he is switched off.

15 WHO: Kirk to Spock. EPISODE: *ST VI: The Undiscovered Country*. CONTEXT: Kirk has just been informed that he will broker peace with his arch-enemies, the Klingons.

16 WHO: Wes to Picard. EPISODE: *Parallels*. CONTEXT: The Enterprise has caused a rupture in dimensional space causing hundreds of parallel universes to converge on the Enterprise's position.

17 WHO: Scotty. EPISODE: *Relics*. CONTEXT: 75 years on, a drunken Scotty – recently rescued from a transporter loop – recreates the bridge of the original Enterprise and gets upset about it.

18 WHO: McCoy. EPISODE: *Devil In The Dark*. CONTEXT: Bones manages to heal a wounded alien rock-eating creature called Horta.

19 WHO: Picard to Yar. EPISODE: *Hide And Q*. CONTEXT: Tasha Yar is upset.

20 WHO: Q to Worf. EPISODE: *Q Who?*. CONTEXT: Q as ever takes pleasure in mocking our occasionally dense Klingon 'chum'.

21 WHO: Scotty. EPISODE: *ST III: The Search for Spock*. CONTEXT: Scotty is unimpressed by the Excelsior.

22 WHO: Data to Picard. EPISODE: *The Naked Now*. CONTEXT: Data is a little inebriated.

23 WHO: Worf to smelly aliens. EPISODE: *The Vengeance Factor*. CONTEXT: A tribe of Gatherers attempt to ambush an away team but are easily pre-empted due to their questionable hygiene.

24 WHO: Captain Jellico. EPISODE: *Chain Of Command 1*. CONTEXT: Jellico has taken command of the Enterprise while Picard is away on a ludicrous secret mission. He immediately begins to make his mark on the ship.

25 WHO: Picard to La Forge. EPISODE: *The Arsenal Of Freedom.* CONTEXT: Picard has left La Forge in charge of the Enterprise while he beams away.

26 WHO: Worf to terrified villagers. EPISODE: *Homeward.* CONTEXT: Geordi's holodeck simulation of their planet is beginning to break up, causing strange objects and weird flashes to appear. Worf tries to placate the villagers.

27 WHO: Riker to Troi. EPISODE: *The Child.* CONTEXT: Riker is stunned by the revelation that Troi has a bun in the oven.

28 WHO: Data to Riker. EPISODE: *A Fistful of Datas.* CONTEXT: Data's programming has intermixed accidentally with a holodeck program of the Wild West. He begins to exhibit strange warning signs.

29 WHO: Klingon to Riker. EPISODE: *A Matter Of Honour.* CONTEXT: Riker, serving as exchange officer on a Klingon vessel, shows distaste for the famed Klingon worm dish. His hilarious Klingon crew mates have a few other suggestions for his nourishment.

30 WHO: Khan to himself, really. EPISODE: *ST II: The Wrath of Khan.* CONTEXT: Khan is mad and intent on exacting his revenge on Kirk.

31 WHO: Data. EPISODE: *The Naked Now.* CONTEXT: Data is still a little inebriated.

32 WHO: Worf to Picard. EPISODE: *Ship In A Bottle.* CONTEXT: Picard extols the virtues of playing with a ship in a bottle as a child and asks an indignant Worf if he did the same.

33 WHO: McCoy. EPISODE: *The Doomsday Machine.* CONTEXT: Bones is called on to perform a miracle.

34 WHO: McCoy. EPISODE: *Friday's Child.* CONTEXT: Bones is called on to perform another miracle.

35 WHO: McCoy. EPISODE: *Mirror, Mirror.* CONTEXT: Bones is called on to perform yet another miracle.

36 WHO: Worf to Vash. EPISODE: *Q-Pid.* CONTEXT: Worf is not unimpressed with Vash's limbs.

37 WHO: Kirk to his son. EPISODE: *ST II: The Wrath of Khan.* CONTEXT: Kirk is explaining the hows and whys of his winning the unwinnable Kobayashi Maru simulation at SFA.

38 WHO: Boothby to Picard. EPISODE: *The First Duty.* CONTEXT: Boothby, the gardener at SFA, is reunited with Picard 30 years on and is, quite frankly, surprised.

39 WHO: Worf to Guinan. EPISODE: *Yesterday's Enterprise.* CONTEXT: Worf has his first taste of prune juice.

40 WHO: Nobody. EPISODE: *None.* CONTEXT: This line has never been said in any Trek episode or film. It's a myth.

41 WHO: Ensign Ro to Riker. EPISODE: *Conundrum.* CONTEXT: The crew have lost their memories. Ro beds Riker. Riker discovers Troi was once his beloved. Ro walks in on the two of them being close. Riker is uncomfortable.

42 WHO: Picard to his officer friends. EPISODE: *All Good Things. . .* CONTEXT: Picard joins them in a game of poker. The penultimate line spoken in TNG. Boo hoo. Sniff. Etc.

43 WHO: Q to Guinan. EPISODE: *Deja Q.* CONTEXT: Q is finding mortality tough.

44 WHO: Riker to Picard. EPISODE: *Skin of Evil.* CONTEXT: The ever descriptive Riker replies thus when Picard asks him what's going on.

45 WHO: Beverly Crusher. EPISODE: *Angel One.* CONTEXT: Bev triumphantly discovers the cure for a nasty virus thing [we had to get one Bev quote in.]

46 WHO: Riker. EPISODE: *Contagion.* CONTEXT: This is as poetic as Riker gets.

47 WHO: Troi. EPISODE: Every single one that I can remember. CONTEXT: She always says this. Always. Always. Always. She's useless.

48 WHO: Worf to Riker. EPISODE: *11001001.* CONTEXT: Worf is geared up and ready for an intership Parisi Squares tournament. Riker has misgivings. Worf does not.

49 WHO: Data to Riker. EPISODE: *ST: Generations*. CONTEXT: Data is having a little trouble controlling his newly installed emotions.

50 WHO: Spock to Kirk. EPISODE: *ST: II The Wrath Of Khan*. CONTEXT: Spock is justifying his death.

WORDS
page 143

1 C. **2** AA. **3** B. **4** BB. **5** N. **6** O. **7** P. **8** D. **9** Q. **10** R. **11** E. **12** CC. **13** F. **14** G. **15** H. **16** S. **17** I. **18** DD. **19** EE. **20** T. **21** FF. **22** U. **23** J. **24** K. **25** V. **26** W. **27** X. **28** L. **29** GG. **30** HH. **31** Y. **32** Z. **33** II. **34** JJ. **35** M. **36** QQ. **37** KK. **38** RR. **39** SS. **40** LL. **41** TT. **42** A. **43** PP. **44** OO. **45** MM. **46** WW. **47** XX. **48** YY. **49** ZZ. **50** NN.

ACADEMY ENTRANCE EXAM
page 148

OVERVIEW
1 Galaxy. **2** Utopia Planetia Shipyards, Mars. **3** Leah Brahms. **4** 2363. **5** Yamoto. **6** Donald Varley. **7** Iconia, The Neutral Zone. **8** a.

STATISTICS
9 Approximately 1012 people. **10** 5000. **11** 800,000 square metres. **12** Warp 9.2. **13** Warp 9.5. **14** Fourteen. Twelve are located on the dorsal and ventral flanks, plus two additional lateral arrays. **15** Three. **16** 3.5 million kilometres. **17** Three. **18** Eight.

GEOGRAPHY
19 Deck 10. **20** Deck 5. **21** Deck 1. **22** Deck 9. **23** Deck 12. **24** Deck 4. **25** Deck 36. **26** Deck 8. **27** Underneath the saucer section. **28** Diplomatic functions. **29** In the brig. **30** Turbolift.

CREW SYSTEMS
31 b. **32** Flight controls. **33** Ship's resources. **34** Defence and internal security. **35** a. **36** Transparent aluminum.

HISTORY
37 Constitution. **38** Captain Christopher Pike. **39** Warp 8. **40** Warp 6. **41** Three. **42** Two. **43** Four hundred and thirty. **44** Fourteen. **45** Primary coloured cartridges. **46** Captain Rachel Garrett . **47** It was destroyed defending the Klingon settlement Khitomer from the Romulans. **48** Ambassador.

STARFLEET REGULATIONS
49 Captain and the First Officer. **50** To jettison the core. **51** Level seven. **52** Level three. **53** Code 1. **54** A declaration of war. **55** Code 47. **56** One. **57** Two and a half. **58** Four. **59** The Prime Directive. **60** Interference with the normal development of any culture or society, especially those technologically less developed. **61** Romulan Ale.

STARFLEET INSTITUTIONS
62 San Francisco. **63** The Daystrom Institute. **64** Intelligence, self-awareness and consciousness. **65** Saturn. **66** The Sandie Hawkins Dance. **67** From the stars, knowledge.

STARFLEET HISTORY
68 Treaty of Algeron. **69** The Federation and the Romulans. **70** Richard Daystrom. **71** By naming the chief scientific research institute after him. **72** It was the location of Starfleet's last stand against the Borg. **73** Thirty-nine. **74** Eleven thousand. **75** Zefram Cochrane.

THE GALAXY
76 The Milky Way. **77** 001. **78** Four. **79** Aplha, Beta, Delta, and Gamma. **80** A quantum singularity. **81** One hundred and fifty. **82** Two – the Klingon and Romulan. **83** The distance between the Earth and the Sun. **84** Cochranes. **85** Because of the Great Barrier which surrounds the galaxy.

STARFLEET TECHNOLOGY

86 Subspace. **87** 25%. **88** With a controlled Barion sweep. **89** 40,000 kms. **90** 1:1 (One to one). **91** TRICK QUESTION. It's still 1:1. **92** Pattern Enhancers. **93** Cloaked space vessels. **94** Dilithium crystals. **95** It is the only substance known to man which is non-reactive to antimatter. **96** The warp containment field. **97** Nacelles. **98** Iso-linear chips. **99** PADDs. **100** Personal Access Display Device. **101** The Universal Translator. **102** A tricorder. **103** Fire weapons. **104** The Romulans. **105** Stun, Kill, Disrupt. **106** The inertia dampers.

THEORETICAL SCIENCE

107 A new form of shield which allows ships to withstand close contact with a sun's corona. **108** A method for travelling at warp speed without a warp drive by 'surfing' on an high-energy particle wave. **109** A tunnel through time and space which can provide relatively instanteous access to distant areas of the cosmos. **110** Dimensional shifting. **111** Because it was found to cause irreparable tissue damage. **112** Be invisible and pass through solid objects. **113** Theoretically, warp 10 requires infinite power and even then the starship would occupy all points of the universe simultaneously. **114** A huge artificial shell built around a sun with landmasses on the inside.

STARFLEET SPACE VESSELS

115 Transmitted identification codes for ships in space. **116** The prefix code. **117** Galaxy, Excelsior, Miranda, Oberth, Nebula, Soyuz, Daedalu, and Ambassador.

GENERAL TECHNOLOGY

118 Synthehol. **119** The Ferengi. **120** Replicators. **121** Quantum and Molecular. **122** A hypospray.

HISTORY

1 e. **2** j. **3** r. **4** d. **5** q. **6** i. **7** p. **8** f. **9** l. **10** a. **11** o. **12** s. **13** n. **14** k. **15** b. **16** c. **17** t. **18** h. **19** m. **20** g.

SCORECARD
for scoring method, see page 7

0 - 200
Pathetic. Terrible. Awful. There are alkaline-based lifeforms invisible to the naked eye on Deneb III which know more about Trek than you do.

201-600
Pretty awful or, frankly, disgusting. Call yourself a Trekker? We've re-evaluated the command structure of this universe and you ain't in it.

601-1000
Cadet Status. Not a bad performance, considering your mother was obviously a Pakled. Go home, revise, and come back later for further sessions.

1001-1400
Ensign Junior Grade. Not bad. Not bad at all. We are pleased with your performance. But it will be a few good decades before your first command

1401-1800
Ensign. Yes, yes. Average peformance. You have some potential, but we suggests a Trekker refresher course just to get you up to scratch.

1801-2200
Lieutenant. Well done. You have performed admirably. You missed a few surface facts but overall you did very well. You have potential.

2201-2600
Lieutenant Commander. Excellent all round performance. We are pleased. You may make 'the chair' one day.

2601-3000
Commander. Just as we expected from a cadet of your calibre. Superb result. You definitely have command potential.

3001-3500
Captain. Outstanding result. We are pleased to offer you captaincy of any ship in the fleet. Your career will be an excellent one, we are sure.

3501-4000

Captain of the Enterprise. Staggering score. Your name will surely go down in the annals of Starfleet history. Take the Enterprise - she is yours. You've earned her.

4000+

Admiral. Blimey. You are definitely TrekMaster calibre. You must have a positronic brain, or more likely, you're a member of the Q continuum. Incredible performance.

4212

TREKMASTER! You've done it! You've have got the maximum possible score. You've cheated haven't you? No one could get this much. Not even Michael Okuda. If you've really got this score, then you must be one of Wesley Crusher's ilk. Expect a visit from the Traveler very soon.